The

Letters of

Mark Twain

Volume 1
1853 - 1866

Mark Twain

The Letters Of Mark Twain, Vol.1
Mark Twain (Samuel Langhorne Clemens)

ARRANGED WITH COMMENT BY ALBERT BIGELOW PAINE

© 1st World Library – Literary Society, 2004
PO Box 2211
Fairfield, IA 52556
www.1stworldlibrary.org
First Edition

LCCN: 2003195047

ISBN: 1-59540-320-5

Purchase *"The Letters of Mark Twain Vol. 1"*
as a traditional bound book at:
www.1stWorldLibrary.org/purchase.asp?ISBN= 1-59540-320-5

1st World Library Literary Society is a nonprofit
organization dedicated to promoting literacy by:

- Creating a free internet library accessible from any
  computer worldwide.
- Hosting writing competitions and offering book
  publishing scholarships.

Readers interested in supporting literacy
through sponsorship, donations or
membership please contact:
literacy@1stworldlibrary.org
Check us out at: www.1stworldlibrary.org

The Letters Of Mark Twain, Vol. 1

contributed by the Charles Family

in support of

1st World Library Literary Society

FOREWORD

Nowhere is the human being more truly revealed than in his letters. Notin literary letters - prepared with care, and the thought of possible publication - but in those letters wrought out of the press of circumstances, and with no idea of print in mind. A collection of such documents, written by one whose life has become of interest to mankind at large, has a value quite aside from literature, in that it reflects in some degree at least the soul of the writer.

The letters of Mark Twain are peculiarly of the revealing sort. He was a man of few restraints and of no affectations. In his correspondence, as in his talk, he spoke what was in his mind, untrammeled by literary conventions.

Necessarily such a collection does not constitute a detailed life story, but is supplementary to it. An extended biography of Mark Twain has already been published. His letters are here gathered for those who wish to pursue the subject somewhat more exhaustively from the strictly personal side. Selections from this correspondence were used in the biography mentioned. Most of these are here reprinted in the belief that an owner of the "Letters" will wish the collection to be reasonably complete.

MARK TWAIN

A BIOGRAPHICAL SUMMARY

SAMUEL LANGHORNE CLEMENS, for nearly half a century known and celebrated as "Mark Twain," was born in Florida, Missouri, on November 30, 1835. He was one of the foremost American philosophers of his day; he was the world's most famous humorist of any day. During the later years of his life he ranked not only as America's chief man of letters, but likewise as her best known and best loved citizen.

The beginnings of that life were sufficiently unpromising. The family was a good one, of old Virginia and Kentucky stock, but its circumstances were reduced, its environment meager and disheartening. The father, John Marshall Clemens - a lawyer by profession, a merchant by vocation - had brought his household to Florida from Jamestown, Tennessee, somewhat after the manner of judge Hawkins as pictured in The Gilded Age. Florida was a small town then, a mere village of twenty-one houses located on Salt River, but judge Clemens, as he was usually called, optimistic and speculative in his temperament, believed in its future. Salt River would be made navigable; Florida would become a metropolis. He established a small business there, and located his family in the humble frame cottage where, five months later, was born a baby boy to whom they gave the name of Samuel - a family name - and added Langhorne, after an old Virginia friend of his father.

The child was puny, and did not make a very sturdy fight for life. Still he weathered along, season after season, and survived two stronger children, Margaret and Benjamin. By 1839 Judge Clemens had lost faith in Florida. He removed his family to Hannibal, and in this Mississippi River town the little lad whom the world was to know as Mark Twain spent his early life. In Tom Sawyer we have a picture of the Hannibal of those days and the atmosphere of his boyhood there.

His schooling was brief and of a desultory kind. It ended one day in 1847, when his father died and it became necessary that each one should help somewhat in the domestic crisis. His brother Orion, ten years his senior, was already a printer by trade. Pamela, his sister; also considerably older, had acquired music, and now took a few pupils. The little boy Sam, at twelve, was apprenticed to a printer named Ament. His wages consisted of his board and clothes - "more board than clothes," as he once remarked to the writer.

He remained with Ament until his brother Orion bought out a small paper in Hannibal in 1850. The paper, in time, was moved into a part of the Clemens home, and the two brothers ran it, the younger setting most of the type. A still younger brother, Henry, entered the office as an apprentice. The Hannibal journal was no great paper from the beginning, and it did not improve with time. Still, it managed to survive - country papers nearly always manage to survive - year after year, bringing in some sort of return. It was on this paper that young Sam Clemens began his writings - burlesque, as a rule, of local characters and conditions - usually published in his brother's absence; generally resulting in trouble on his return. Yet they made the paper sell, and if Orion had but realized his brother's talent he might have turned it into capital even then.

In 1853 (he was not yet eighteen) Sam Clemens grew tired of his limitations and pined for the wider horizon of the world. He gave out to his family that he was going to St. Louis, but he kept on to New York, where a World's Fair was then going on. In New York he found employment at his trade, and during the hot months of 1853 worked in a printing-office in Cliff Street. By and by he went to Philadelphia, where he worked a brief time; made a trip to Washington, and presently set out for the West again, after an absence of more than a year.

Onion, meanwhile, had established himself at Muscatine, Iowa, but soon after removed to Keokuk, where the brothers were once more together, till following their trade. Young Sam Clemens remained in Keokuk until the winter of 1856-57, when he caught a touch of the South-American fever then prevalent; and decided to go to Brazil. He left Keokuk for Cincinnati, worked that winter in a printing-office there, and in April took the little steamer, Paul Jones, for New Orleans, where he expected to find a South-American vessel. In Life on the Mississippi we have his story of how he met Horace Bixby and decided to become a pilot instead of a South American adventurer - jauntily setting himself the stupendous task of learning the twelve hundred miles of the Mississippi River between St. Louis and New Orleans - of knowing it as exactly and as unfailingly, even in the dark, as one knows the way to his own features. It seems incredible to those who knew Mark Twain in his later years - dreamy, unpractical, and indifferent to details - that he could have acquired so vast a store of minute facts as were required by that task. Yet within eighteen months he had become not only a pilot, but one of the best and most careful pilots on the river, intrusted with some of the largest and most valuable steamers. He continued in that profession for two and a half years longer, and during that time met with no disaster that cost his owners a single dollar for damage.

Then the war broke out. South Carolina seceded in December, 1860 and other States followed. Clemens was in New Orleans in January, 1861, when Louisiana seceded, and his boat was put into the Confederate service and sent up the Red River. His occupation gone, he took steamer for the North - the last one before the blockade closed. A blank cartridge was fired at them from Jefferson Barracks when they reached St. Louis, but they did not understand the signal, and kept on. Presently a shell carried away part of the pilot-house and considerably disturbed its inmates. They realized, then, that war had really begun.

In those days Clemens's sympathies were with the South. He hurried up to Hannibal and enlisted with a company of young fellows who were recruiting with the avowed purpose of "throwing off the yoke of the invader." They were ready for the field, presently, and set out in good order, a sort of nondescript cavalry detachment, mounted on animals more picturesque than beautiful. Still, it was a resolute band, and might have done very well, only it rained a good deal, which made soldiering disagreeable and hard. Lieutenant Clemens resigned at the end of two weeks, and decided to go to Nevada with Orion, who was a Union abolitionist and had received an appointment from Lincoln as Secretary of the new Territory.

In 'Roughing It' Mark Twain gives us the story of the overland journey made by the two brothers, and a picture of experiences at the other end - true in aspect, even if here and there elaborated in detail. He was Orion's private secretary, but there was no private-secretary work to do, and no salary attached to the position. The incumbent presently went to mining, adding that to his other trades.

He became a professional miner, but not a rich one. He was at Aurora, California, in the Esmeralda district, skimping along, with not much to eat and less to wear, when he was summoned by Joe Goodman, owner and editor of the Virginia City Enterprise, to come up and take the local editorship of that paper. He had been contributing sketches to it now and then, under the pen, name of "Josh," and Goodman, a man of fine literary instincts, recognized a talent full of possibilities. This was in the late summer of 1862. Clemens walked one hundred and thirty miles over very bad roads to take the job, and arrived way-worn and travel-stained. He began on a salary of twenty-five dollars a week, picking up news items here and there, and contributing occasional sketches, burlesques, hoaxes, and the like. When the Legislature convened at Carson City he was sent down to report it, and then, for the first time, began signing his articles "Mark Twain," a river term, used in making soundings, recalled from his piloting days. The name presently became known up and down the Pacific coast. His articles were, copied and commented upon. He was recognized as one of the foremost among a little coterie of overland writers, two of whom, Mark Twain and Bret Harte, were soon to acquire a world-wide fame.

He left Carson City one day, after becoming involved in a duel, the result of an editorial squib written in Goodman's absence, and went across the Sierras to San Francisco. The duel turned out farcically enough, but the Nevada law, which regarded even a challenge or its acceptance as a felony, was an inducement to his departure. Furthermore, he had already aspired to a wider field of literary effort. He attached himself to the Morning Call, and wrote occasionally for one or two literary papers - the Golden Era and the Californian - prospering well enough during the better part of the year. Bret Harte and the rest of the little Pacific-slope group were also on the staff of these papers, and for a time, at least, the new school of American humor mustered in San Francisco.

The connection with the Call was not congenial. In due course it came to a natural end, and Mark Twain arranged to do a daily San Francisco letter for his old paper, the Enterprise. The Enterprise letters stirred up trouble. They criticized the police of San Francisco so severely that the officials found means of making the writer's life there difficult and comfortless. With Jim Gillis, brother of a printer of whom he was fond, and who had been the indirect cause of his troubles, he went up into Calaveras County, to a cabin on jackass Hill. Jim Gillis, a lovable, picturesque character (the Truthful James of Bret Harte), owned mining claims. Mark Twain decided to spend his vacation in pocket-mining, and soon added that science to his store of knowledge. It was a halcyon, happy three months that he lingered there, but did not make his fortune; he only laid the corner-stone.

They tried their fortune at Angel's Camp, a place well known to readers of Bret Harte. But it rained pretty steadily, and they put in most of their time huddled around the single stove of the dingy hotel of Angel's, telling yarns. Among the stories was one told by a dreary narrator named Ben Coon. It was about a frog that had been trained to jump, but failed to win a wager because the owner of a rival frog had surreptitiously loaded him with shot. The story had been circulated among the camps, but Mark Twain had never heard it until then. The tale and the tiresome fashion of its telling amused him. He made notes to remember it.

Their stay in Angel's Camp came presently to an end. One day, when the mining partners were following the specks of gold that led to a pocket somewhere up the hill, a chill, dreary rain set in. Jim, as usual was washing, and Clemens was carrying water. The "color" became better and better as they ascended, and Gillis, possessed with the mining passion, would have gone on, regardless of the rain. Clemens, however, protested, and declared that each pail of water was his last. Finally he said, in his deliberate drawl:

"Jim, I won't carry any more water. This work is too disagreeable. Let's go to the house and wait till it clears up."

Gillis had just taken out a pan of earth. "Bring one more pail, Sam," he pleaded.

"I won't do it, Jim! Not a drop! Not if I knew there was a million dollars in that pan!"

They left the pan standing there and went back to Angel's Camp. The rain continued and they returned to jackass Hill without visiting their claim again. Meantime the rain had washed away the top of the pan of earth left standing on the slope above Angel's, and exposed a handful of nuggets-pure gold. Two strangers came along and, observing it, had sat down to wait until the thirty-day claim-notice posted by Jim Gillis should expire. They did not mind the rain - not with that gold in sight - and the minute the thirty days were up they followed the lead a few pans further, and took out-some say ten, some say twenty, thousand dollars. It was a good pocket. Mark Twain missed it by one pail of water. Still, it is just as well, perhaps, when one remembers The Jumping Frog.

Matters having quieted down in San Francisco, he returned and took up his work again. Artemus Ward, whom he had met in Virginia City, wrote him for something to use in his (Ward's) new book. Clemens sent the frog story, but he had been dilatory in preparing it, and when it reached New York, Carleton, the publisher, had Ward's book about ready for the press. It did not seem worth while to Carleton to include the frog story, and handed it over to Henry Clapp, editor of the Saturday Press - a perishing sheet- saying:

"Here, Clapp, here's something you can use."

The story appeared in the Saturday Press of November 18, 1865. According to the accounts of that time it set all New York in a roar, which annoyed, rather than gratified, its author. He had thought very little of it, indeed, yet had been wondering why some of his more highly regarded work had not found fuller recognition.

But The Jumping Frog did not die. Papers printed it

and reprinted it, and it was translated into foreign tongues. The name of "Mark Twain" became known as the author of that sketch, and the two were permanently associated from the day of its publication.

Such fame as it brought did not yield heavy financial return. Its author continued to win a more or less precarious livelihood doing miscellaneous work, until March, 1866, when he was employed by the Sacramento Union to contribute a series of letters from the Sandwich Islands. They were notable letters, widely read and freely copied, and the sojourn there was a generally fortunate one. It was during his stay in the islands that the survivors of the wrecked vessel, the Hornet, came in, after long privation at sea. Clemens was sick at the time, but Anson Burlingame, who was in Honolulu, on the way to China, had him carried in a cot to the hospital, where he could interview the surviving sailors and take down their story. It proved a great "beat" for the Union, and added considerably to its author's prestige. On his return to San Francisco he contributed an article on the Hornet disaster to Harper's Magazine, and looked forward to its publication as a beginning of a real career. But, alas! when it appeared the printer and the proof-reader had somehow converted "Mark Twain" into "Mark Swain," and his dreams perished.

Undecided as to his plans, he was one day advised by a friend to deliver a lecture. He was already known as an entertaining talker, and his adviser judged his possibilities well. In Roughing It we find the story of that first lecture and its success. He followed it with other lectures up and down the Coast. He had added one more profession to his intellectual stock in trade.

Mark Twain, now provided with money, decided to pay a visit to his people. He set out for the East in December, 1866, via Panama, arriving in New York in January. A few days later he was with his mother, then living with his sister, in St. Louis. A little later he lectured in Keokuk, and in Hannibal, his old home.

It was about this time that the first great Mediterranean steamship excursion began to be exploited. No such ocean picnic had ever been planned before, and it created a good deal of interest East and West. Mark Twain heard of it and wanted to go. He wrote to friends on the 'Alta California,' of San Francisco, and the publishers of that paper had sufficient faith to advance the money for his passage, on the under-standing that he was to contribute frequent letters, at twenty dollars apiece. It was a liberal offer, as rates went in those days, and a godsend in the fullest sense of the word to Mark Twain.

Clemens now hurried to New York in order to be there in good season for the sailing date, which was in June. In New York he met Frank Fuller, whom he had known as territorial Governor of Utah, an energetic and enthusiastic admirer of the Western humorist. Fuller immediately proposed that Clemens give a lecture in order to establish his reputation on the Atlantic coast. Clemens demurred, but Fuller insisted, and engaged Cooper Union for the occasion. Not many tickets were sold. Fuller, however, always ready for an emergency, sent out a flood of complimentaries to the school-teachers of New York and adjacent territory, and the house was crammed. It turned out to be a notable event. Mark Twain was at his best that night; the audience laughed until, as some of them declared when the lecture was over, they were too weak to leave their seats. His success as a lecturer was assured.

The Quaker City was the steamer selected for the great oriental tour. It sailed as advertised, June 8, 1867, and was absent five months, during which Mark Twain contributed regularly to the 'Alta-California', and wrote several letters for the New York Tribune. They were read and copied everywhere. They preached a new gospel in travel literature - a gospel of seeing with an overflowing honesty; a gospel of sincerity in according praise to whatever he considered genuine, and ridicule to the things believed to be shams. It was a gospel that Mark Twain continued to preach during his whole career. It became, in fact, his chief literary message to the world, a world ready for that message.

He returned to find himself famous. Publishers were ready with plans for collecting the letters in book form. The American Publishing Company, of Hartford, proposed a volume, elaborately illustrated, to be sold by subscription. He agreed with them as to terms, and went to Washington' to prepare copy. But he could not work quietly there, and presently was back in San Francisco, putting his book together, lecturing occasionally, always to crowded houses. He returned in August, 1868, with the manuscript of the Innocents Abroad, and that winter, while his book was being manufactured, lectured throughout the East and Middle West, making his headquarters in Hartford, and in Elmira, New York.

He had an especial reason for going to Elmira. On the Quaker City he had met a young man by the name of Charles Langdon, and one day, in the Bay of Smyrna, had seen a miniature of the boy's sister, Olivia Langdon, then a girl of about twenty-two. He fell in love with that picture, and still more deeply in love with the original when he met her in New York on his return. The Langdon home was in Elmira, and it was for this reason that as time passed he frequently sojourned there. When the proofs of the Innocents Abroad were sent him he took them along, and he and sweet "Livy" Langdon read them together. What he lacked in those days in literary delicacy she detected, and together they pruned it away. She became his editor that winter - a position which she held until her death.

The book was published in July, 1869, and its success was immediate and abundant. On his wedding-day, February 2, 1870, Clemens received a check from his publishers for more than four thousand dollars, royalty accumulated during the three months preceding. The sales soon amounted to more than fifty thousand copies, and had increased to very nearly one hundred thousand at the end of the first three years. It was a book of travel, its lowest price three dollars and fifty cents. Even with our increased reading population no such sale is found for a book of that description to-day. And the Innocents Abroad holds its place - still outsells every other book in its particular field. [This in 1917. D.W.]

Mark Twain now decided to settle down. He had bought an interest in the Express, of Buffalo, New York, and took up his residence in that city in a house presented to the young couple by Mr. Langdon. It did not prove a fortunate beginning. Sickness, death, and trouble of many kinds put a blight on the happiness of their first married year and gave, them a distaste for the home in which they had made such a promising start. A baby boy, Langdon Clemens, came along in

November, but he was never a strong child. By the end of the following year the Clemenses had arranged for a residence in Hartford, temporary at first, later made permanent. It was in Hartford that little Langdon died, in 1872.

Clemens, meanwhile, had sold out his interest in the Express, severed his connection with the Galaxy, a magazine for which he was doing a department each month, and had written a second book for the American Publishing Company, Roughing It, published in 1872. In August of the same year he made a trip to London, to get material for a book on England, but was too much sought after, too continuously feted, to do any work. He went alone, but in November returned with the purpose of taking Mrs. Clemens and the new baby, Susy, to England the following spring. They sailed in April, 1873, and spent a good portion of the year in England and Scotland. They returned to America in November, and Clemens hurried back to London alone to deliver a notable series of lectures under the management of George Dolby, formerly managing agent for Charles Dickens. For two months Mark Twain lectured steadily to London audiences - the big Hanover Square rooms always filled. He returned to his family in January, 1874.

Meantime, a home was being built for them in Hartford, and in the autumn of 1874 they took up residence in ita happy residence, continued through seventeen years - well-nigh perfect years. Their summers they spent in Elmira, on Quarry Farm - a beautiful hilltop, the home of Mrs. Clemens's sister. It was in Elmira that much of Mark Twain's literary work was done. He had a special study there, some distance from the house, where he loved to work out his fancies and put them into visible form.

It was not so easy to work at Hartford; there was too much going on. The Clemens home was a sort of general headquarters for literary folk, near and far, and for distinguished foreign visitors of every sort. Howells and Aldrich used it as their half-way station between Boston and New York, and every foreign notable who visited America made a pilgrimage to Hartford to see Mark Twain. Some even went as far as Elmira, among them Rudyard Kipling, who recorded his visit in a chapter of his American Notes. Kipling declared he had come all the way from India to see Mark Twain.

Hartford had its own literary group. Mrs. Harriet Beecher Stowe lived near the Clemens home; also Charles Dudley Warner. The Clemens and Warner families were constantly associated, and The Gilded Age, published in 1873, resulted from the friendship of Warner and Mark Twain. The character of Colonel Sellers in that book has become immortal, and it is a character that only Mark Twain could create, for, though drawn from his mother's cousin, James Lampton, it embodies - and in no very exaggerated degree - characteristics that were his own. The tendency to make millions was always imminent; temptation was always hard to resist. Money-making schemes are continually being placed before men of means and prominence, and Mark Twain, to the day of his death, found such schemes fatally attractive.

It was because of the Sellers characteristics in him that he invested in a typesetting-machine which cost him nearly two hundred thousand dollars and helped to wreck his fortunes by and by. It was because of this characteristic that he invested in numberless schemes of lesser importance, but no less disastrous in the end. His one successful commercial venture was his association with Charles L. Webster in the publication of the Grant Memoirs, of which enough copies were sold to pay a royalty of more than four hundred thousand dollars to Grant's widow - the largest royalty ever paid from any single publication. It saved the Grant family from poverty. Yet even this triumph was a misfortune to Mark Twain, for it led to scores of less profitable book ventures and eventual disaster.

Meanwhile he had written and published a number of books. Tom Sawyer, The Prince and the Pauper, Life on the Mississippi, Huckleberry Finn, and A Connecticut Yankee in King Arthur's Court were among the volumes that had entertained the world and inspired it with admiration and love for their author. In 1878-79 he had taken his family to Europe, where they spent their time in traveling over the Continent. It was during this period that he was joined by his intimate friend, the Rev. Joseph H. Twichell, of Hartford, and the two made a journey, the story of which is told in A Tramp Abroad.

In 1891 the Hartford house was again closed, this time indefinitely, and the family, now five in number, took up residence in Berlin. The typesetting-machine and the unfortunate publishing venture were drawing heavily on the family finances at this period, and the cost of the Hartford establishment was too great to be maintained. During the next three years he was distracted by the financial struggle which ended in April, 1894, with the failure of Charles L. Webster & Co. Mark Twain now found himself bankrupt, and nearly one hundred thousand dollars in debt. It had been a losing fight, with this bitter ending always in view; yet during this period of hard, hopeless effort he had written a large portion of the book which of all his works will perhaps survive the longest - his tender and beautiful story of Joan of Arc. All his life Joan had been his favorite character in the world's history, and during those trying months and years of the early nineties - in Berlin, in Florence, in Paris - he was conceiving and putting his picture of that gentle girl-warrior into perfect literary form. It was published in Harper's Magazine - anonymously, because, as he said, it would not have been received seriously had it appeared over his own name. The authorship was presently recognized. Exquisitely, reverently, as the story was told, it had in it the, touch of quaint and gentle humor which could only have been given to it by Mark Twain.

It was only now and then that Mark Twain lectured during these years. He had made a reading tour with George W. Cable during the winter of 1884-85, but he abominated the platform, and often vowed he would never appear before an audience again. Yet, in 1895, when he was sixty years old, he decided to rebuild his fortunes by making a reading tour around the world. It was not required of him to pay his debts in full. The creditors were willing to accept fifty per cent. of the liabilities, and had agreed to a settlement on that basis. But this did not satisfy Mrs. Clemens, and it did not satisfy him. They decided to pay dollar for dollar. They sailed for America, and in July, 1895, set out from Elmira on the long trail across land and sea. Mrs. Clemens, and Clara Clemens, joined this pilgrimage, Susy and Jean Clemens remaining at Elmira with their aunt. Looking out of the car windows, the travelers saw Susy waving them an adieu. It was a picture they would long remember.

The reading tour was one of triumph. High prices and crowded houses prevailed everywhere. The author-reader visited Australia, New Zealand, India, Ceylon, South Africa, arriving in England, at last, with the money and material which would pay off the heavy burden of debt and make him once more free before the world. And in that hour of triumph came the heavy blow. Susy Clemens, never very strong, had been struck down. The first cable announced her illness. The mother and Clara sailed at once. Before they were half-way across the ocean a second cable announced that Susy was dead. The father had to meet and endure the heartbreak alone; he could not reach America, in time for the burial. He remained in England, and was joined there by the sorrowing family.

They passed that winter in London, where he worked at the story of his travels, Following the Equator, the proofs of which he read the next summer in Switzerland. The returns from it, and from his reading venture, wiped away Mark Twain's indebtedness and made him free. He could go back to America; as he said, able to look any man in the face again.

Yet he did not go immediately. He could live more economically abroad, and economy was still necessary. The family spent two winters in Vienna, and their apartments there constituted a veritable court where the world's notables gathered. Another winter in England followed, and then, in the latter part of 1900, they went home - that is, to America. Mrs. Clemens never could bring herself to return to Hartford, and never saw their home there again.

Mark Twain's return to America, was in the nature of a national event. Wherever he appeared throngs turned out to bid him welcome. Mighty banquets were planned in his honor.

In a house at 14 West Tenth Street, and in a beautiful place at Riverdale, on the Hudson, most of the next three years were passed. Then Mrs. Clemens's health failed, and in the autumn of 1903 the family went to Florence for her benefit. There, on the 5th of June, 1904, she died. They brought her back and laid her beside Susy, at Elmira. That winter the family took up residence at 21 Fifth Avenue, New York, and remained there until the completion of Stormfield, at Redding, Connecticut, in 1908.

In his later life Mark Twain was accorded high academic honors. Already, in 1888, he had received from Yale College the degree of Master of Arts, and the same college made him a Doctor of Literature in 1901. A year later the university of his own State, at Columbia, Missouri, conferred the same degree, and then, in 1907, came the crowning honor, when venerable Oxford tendered him the doctor's robe.

"I don't know why they should give me a degree like that," he said, quaintly. "I never doctored any literature - I wouldn't know how."

He had thought never to cross the ocean again, but he declared he would travel to Mars and back, if necessary, to get that Oxford degree. He appreciated its full meaning-recognition by the world's foremost institution of learning of the achievements of one who had no learning of the institutionary kind. He sailed in

June, and his sojourn in England was marked by a continuous ovation. His hotel was besieged by callers. Two secretaries were busy nearly twenty hours a day attending to visitors and mail. When he appeared on the street his name went echoing in every direction and the multitudes gathered. On the day when he rose, in his scarlet robe and black mortar-board, to receive his degree (he must have made a splendid picture in that dress, with his crown of silver hair), the vast assembly went wild. What a triumph, indeed, for the little Missouri printer-boy! It was the climax of a great career.

Mark Twain's work was always of a kind to make people talk, always important, even when it was mere humor. Yet it was seldom that; there was always wisdom under it, and purpose, and these things gave it dynamic force and enduring life. Some of his aphorisms - so quaint in form as to invite laughter - are yet fairly startling in their purport. His paraphrase, "When in doubt, tell the truth," is of this sort. "Frankness is a jewel; only the young can afford it," he once said to the writer, apropos of a little girl's remark. His daily speech was full of such things. The secret of his great charm was his great humanity and the gentle quaintness and sincerity of his utterance.

His work did not cease when the pressing need of money came to an end. He was full of ideas, and likely to begin a new article or story at any time. He wrote and published a number of notable sketches, articles, stories, even books, during these later years, among them that marvelous short story - "The Man That Corrupted Hadleyburg." In that story, as in most of his later work, he proved to the world that he was much more than a humorist - that he was, in fact, a great teacher, moralist, philosopher - the greatest, perhaps, of his age.

His life at Stormfield - he had never seen the place until the day of his arrival, June 18, 1908 - was a peaceful and serene old age. Not that he was really old; he never was that. His step, his manner, his point of view, were all and always young. He was fond of children and frequently had them about him. He delighted in games - especially in billiards - and in building the house at Stormfield the billiard-room was first considered. He had a genuine passion for the sport; without it his afternoon was not complete. His mornings he was likely to pass in bed, smoking - he was always smoking - and attending to his correspondence and reading. History and the sciences interested him, and his bed was strewn with biographies and stories of astronomical and geological research. The vastness of distances and periods always impressed him. He had no head for figures, but he would labor for hours over scientific calculations, trying to compass them and to grasp their gigantic import. I remember once finding him highly elated over the fact that he had figured out for himself the length in hours and minutes of a "light year." He showed me the pages covered with figures, and was more proud of them than if they had been the pages of an immortal story. Then we played billiards, but even his favorite game could not make him altogether forget his splendid achievement.

It was on the day before Christmas, 1909, that heavy bereavement once more came into the life of Mark Twain. His daughter Jean, long subject to epileptic attacks, was seized with a convulsion while in her bath and died before assistance reached her. He was dazed by the suddenness of the blow. His philosophy sustained him. He was glad, deeply glad for the beautiful girl that had been released.

"I never greatly envied anybody but the dead," he said, when he had looked at her. "I always envy the dead."

The coveted estate of silence, time's only absolute gift, it was the one benefaction he had ever considered worth while.

Yet the years were not unkindly to Mark Twain. They brought him sorrow, but they brought him likewise the capacity and opportunity for large enjoyment, and at the last they laid upon him a kind of benediction. Naturally impatient, he grew always more gentle, more generous, more tractable and considerate as the seasons passed. His final days may be said to have been spent in the tranquil light of a summer afternoon.

His own end followed by a few months that of his daughter. There were already indications that his heart was seriously affected, and soon after Jean's death he sought the warm climate of Bermuda. But his malady made rapid progress, and in April he returned to Stormfield. He died there just a week later, April 21, 1910.

Any attempt to designate Mark Twain's place in the world's literary history would be presumptuous now. Yet I cannot help thinking that he will maintain his supremacy in the century that produced him. I think so because, of all the writers of that hundred years, his work was the most human his utterances went most surely to the mark. In the long analysis of the ages it is the truth that counts, and he never approximated, never compromised, but pronounced those absolute verities to which every human being of whatever rank must instantly respond.

His understanding of subjective human nature - the vast, unwritten life within - was simply amazing. Such knowledge he acquired at the fountainhead - that is, from himself. He recognized in himself an extreme example of the human being with all the attributes of power and of weakness, and he made his exposition complete.

The world will long miss Mark Twain; his example and his teaching will be neither ignored nor forgotten. Genius defies the laws of perspective and looms larger as it recedes. The memory of Mark Twain remains to us a living and intimate presence that today, even more than in life, constitutes a stately moral bulwark reared against hypocrisy and superstition - a mighty national menace to sham.

I. EARLY LETTERS, 1853.

NEW YORK AND PHILADELPHIA

We have no record of Mark Twain's earliest letters. Very likely they were soiled pencil notes, written to some school sweetheart - to "Becky Thatcher," perhaps - and tossed across at lucky moments, or otherwise, with happy or disastrous results. One of those smudgy, much-folded school notes of the Tom Sawyer period would be priceless to-day, and somewhere among forgotten keepsakes it may exist, but we shall not be likely to find it. No letter of his boyhood, no scrap of his earlier writing, has come to light except his penciled name, SAM CLEMENS, laboriously inscribed on the inside of a small worn purse that once held his meager, almost non-existent wealth. He became a printer's apprentice at twelve, but as he received no salary, the need of a purse could not have been urgent. He must have carried it pretty steadily, however, from its appearance - as a kind of symbol of hope, maybe - a token of that Sellers-optimism which dominated his early life, and was never entirely subdued.

No other writing of any kind has been preserved from Sam Clemens's boyhood, none from that period of his youth when he had served his apprenticeship and was a capable printer on his brother's paper, a contributor to it when occasion served. Letters and manuscripts of those days have vanished - even his contributions in printed form are unobtainable. It is not believed that a single number of Orion Clemens's paper, the Hannibal Journal, exists to-day.

It was not until he was seventeen years old that Sam Clemens wrote a letter any portion of which has survived. He was no longer in Hannibal. Orion's unprosperous enterprise did not satisfy him. His wish to earn money and to see the world had carried him first to St. Louis, where his sister Pamela was living, then to New York City, where a World's Fair in a Crystal Palace was in progress. The letter tells of a visit to this great exhibition. It is not complete, and the fragment bears no date, but it was written during the summer of 1853.

Fragment of a letter from Sam L. Clemens to his sister Pamela Moffett, in St. Louis, summer of 1853:

. . . From the gallery (second floor) you have a glorious sight - the flags of the different countries represented, the lofty dome, glittering jewelry, gaudy tapestry, &c., with the busy crowd passing to and fro - tis a perfect fairy palace - beautiful beyond description.

The Machinery department is on the main floor, but I cannot enumerate any of it on account of the lateness of the hour (past 8 o'clock.) It would take more than a week to examine everything on exhibition; and as I was only in a little over two hours tonight, I only glanced at about one-third of the articles; and having a poor memory; I have enumerated scarcely any of even the principal objects. The visitors to the Palace average 6,000 daily - double the population of Hannibal. The price of admission being 50 cents, they take in about $3,000.

The Latting Observatory (height about 280 feet) is near the Palace - from it you can obtain a grand view of the city and the country round. The Croton Aqueduct, to supply the city with water, is the greatest wonder yet. Immense sewers are laid across the bed of the Hudson River, and pass through the country to Westchester county, where a whole river is turned from its course, and brought to New York. From the reservoir in the city to the Westchester county reservoir, the distance is thirty-eight miles! and if necessary, they could supply every family in New York with one hundred barrels of water per day!

I am very sorry to learn that Henry has been sick. He ought to go to the country and take exercise; for he is not half so healthy as Ma thinks he is. If he had my walking to do, he would be another boy entirely. Four times every day I walk a little over one mile; and working hard all day, and walking four miles, is exercise - I am used to it, now, though, and it is no trouble. Where is it Orion's going to? Tell Ma my promises are faithfully kept, and if I have my health I will take her to Ky. in the spring - I shall save money for this. Tell Jim and all the rest of them to write, and give me all the news. I am sorry to hear such bad news from Will and Captain Bowen. I shall write to Will soon. The Chatham-square Post Office and the Broadway office too, are out of my way, and I always go to the General Post Office; so you must write the direction of my letters plain, "New York City, N. Y.," without giving the street or anything of the kind, or they may go to some of the other offices. (It has just struck 2 A.M. and I always get up at 6, and am at work at 7.) You ask me where I spend my evenings. Where would you suppose, with a free printers' library containing more than 4,000 volumes within a quarter of a mile of me, and nobody at home to talk to? I shall write to Ella soon. Write soon

Truly your Brother

SAM.

P. S. I have written this by a light so dim that you nor Ma could not read by it.

He was lodging in a mechanics' cheap boarding-house in Duane Street, and we may imagine the bareness of his room, the feeble poverty of his lamp.

"Tell Ma my promises are faithfully kept." It was the day when he had left Hannibal. His mother, Jane Clemens, a resolute, wiry woman of forty-nine, had put together his few belongings. Then, holding up a little Testament:

"I want you to take hold of the end of this, Sam," she said, "and make me a promise. I want you to repeat after me these words: 'I do solemnly swear that I will not throw a card, or drink a drop of liquor while I am gone.'"

It was this oath, repeated after her, that he was keeping faithfully. The Will Bowen mentioned is a former playmate, one of Tom Sawyer's outlaw band.

He had gone on the river to learn piloting with an elder brother, the "Captain." What the bad news was is no longer remembered, but it could not have been very serious, for the Bowen boys remained on the river for many years. "Ella" was Samuel Clemens's cousin and one-time sweetheart, Ella Creel. "Jim" was Jim Wolfe, an apprentice in Orion's office, and the hero of an adventure which long after Mark Twain wrote under the title of, "Jim Wolfe and the Cats."

There is scarcely a hint of the future Mark Twain in this early letter. It is the letter of a boy of seventeen who is beginning to take himself rather seriously - who, finding himself for the first time far from home and equal to his own responsibilities, is willing to carry the responsibility of others. Henry, his brother, three years younger, had been left in the printing-office with Orion, who, after a long, profitless fight, is planning to remove from Hannibal. The young traveler is concerned as to the family outlook, and will furnish advice if invited. He feels the approach of prosperity, and will take his mother on a long-coveted trip to her old home in the spring. His evenings? Where should he spend them, with a free library of four thousand volumes close by? It is distinctly a youthful letter, a bit pretentious, and wanting in the spontaneity and humor of a later time. It invites comment, now, chiefly because it is the first surviving document in the long human story.

He was working in the printing-office of John A. Gray and Green, on Cliff Street, and remained there through the summer. He must have written more than once during this period, but the next existing letter - also to Sister Pamela - was written in October. It is perhaps a shade more natural in tone than the earlier example, and there is a hint of Mark Twain in the first paragraph.

To Mrs. Moffett, in St. Louis:

NEW YORK . . . , Oct. Saturday '53.

MY DEAR SISTER, - I have not written to any of the family for some time, from the fact, firstly, that I didn't know where they were, and secondly, because I have been fooling myself with the idea that I was going to leave New York every day for the last two weeks. I have taken a liking to the abominable place, and every time I get ready to leave, I put it off a day or so, from some unaccountable cause. It is as hard on my conscience to leave New York, as it was easy to leave Hannibal. I think I shall get off Tuesday, though.

Edwin Forrest has been playing, for the last sixteen days, at the Broadway Theatre, but I never went to see him till last night. The play was the "Gladiator." I did not like parts of it much, but other portions were really splendid. In the latter part of the last act, where the "Gladiator" (Forrest) dies at his brother's feet, (in all the fierce pleasure of gratified revenge,) the man's whole soul seems absorbed in the part he is playing; and it is really startling to see him. I am sorry I did not see him play "Damon and Pythias" the former character being his greatest. He appears in Philadelphia on Monday night.

I have not received a letter from home lately, but got a "'Journal'" the other day, in which I see the office has been sold. I suppose Ma, Orion and Henry are in St. Louis now. If Orion has no other project in his head, he ought to take the contract for getting out some weekly paper, if he cannot get a foremanship. Now, for such a paper as the "Presbyterian" (containing about 60,000, - [Sixty thousand ems, type measurement.]) he could get $20 or $25 per week, and he and Henry could easily do the work; nothing to do but set the type and make up the forms....

If my letters do not come often, you need not bother yourself about me; for if you have a brother nearly eighteen years of age, who is not able to take care of himself a few miles from home, such a brother is not worth one's thoughts: and if I don't manage to take care of No. 1, be assured you will never know it. I am not afraid, however; I shall ask favors from no one, and endeavor to be (and shall be) as "independent as a wood-sawyer's clerk."

I never saw such a place for military companies as New York. Go on the street when you will, you are sure to meet a company in full uniform, with all the usual appendages of drums, fifes, &c. I saw a large company of soldiers of 1812 the other day, with a '76 veteran scattered here and there in the ranks. And as I passed through one of the parks lately, I came upon a company of boys on parade. Their uniforms were neat, and their muskets about half the common size. Some of them were not more than seven or eight years of age; but had evidently been well-drilled.

Passage to Albany (160 miles) on the finest steamers that ply' the Hudson, is now 25 cents - cheap enough, but is generally cheaper than that in the summer.

I want you to write as soon as I tell you where to direct your letter. I would let you know now, if I knew myself. I may perhaps be here a week longer; but I cannot tell. When you write tell me the whereabouts of the family. My love to Mr. Moffett and Ella. Tell Ella I intend to write to her soon, whether she wants me to nor not.

Truly your Brother,

SAML L. CLEMENS.

He was in Philadelphia when he wrote the nest letter that has come down to us, and apparently satisfied with the change. It is a letter to Orion Clemens, who had disposed of his paper, but evidently was still in Hannibal. An extended description of a trip to Fairmount Park is omitted because of its length, its chief interest being the tendency it shows to descriptive writing - the field in which he would make his first great fame. There is, however, no hint of humor, and only a mild suggestion of the author of the Innocents Abroad in this early attempt. The letter as here given is otherwise complete, the omissions being indicated.

To Orion Clemens, in Hannibal:

PHILADELPHIA, PA. Oct. 26,1853.

MY DEAR BROTHER, - It was at least two weeks before I left New York, that I received my last letter from home: and since then, not a word have I heard from any of you. And now, since I think of it, it wasn't a letter, either, but the last number of the "Daily Journal," saying that that paper was sold, and I very naturally supposed from that, that the family had disbanded, and taken up winter quarters in St. Louis. Therefore, I have been writing to Pamela, till I've tired of it, and have received no answer. I have been writing for the last two or three weeks, to send Ma some money, but devil take me if I knew where she was, and so the money has slipped out of my pocket somehow or other, but I have a dollar left, and a good deal owing to me, which will be paid next Monday. I shall enclose the dollar in this letter, and you can hand it to her. I know it's a small amount, but then it will buy her a handkerchief, and at the same time serve as a specimen of the kind of stuff we are paid with in Philadelphia, for you see it's against the law, in Pennsylvania, to keep or pass a bill of less denomination than $5. I have only seen two or three bank bills since I have been in the State. On Monday the hands are paid off in sparkling gold, fresh from the Mint; so your dreams are not troubled with the fear of having doubtful money in your pocket.

I am subbing at the Inquirer office. One man has engaged me to work for him every Sunday till the first of next April, (when I shall return home to take Ma to

Ky;) and another has engaged my services for the 24th of next month; and if I want it, I can get subbing every night of the week. I go to work at 7 o'clock in the evening, and work till 3 o'clock the next morning. I can go to the theatre and stay till 12 o'clock and then go to the office, and get work from that till 3 the next morning; when I go to bed, and sleep till 11 o'clock, then get up and loaf the rest of the day. The type is mostly agate and minion, with some bourgeois; and when one gets a good agate take, - ["Agate," "minion," etc., sizes of type; "take," a piece of work. Type measurement is by ems, meaning the width of the letter 'm'.] - he is sure to make money. I made $2.50 last Sunday, and was laughed at by all the hands, the poorest of whom sets 11,000 on Sunday; and if I don't set 10,000, at least, next Sunday, I'll give them leave to laugh as much as they want to. Out of the 22 compositors in this office, 12 at least, set 15,000 on Sunday.

Unlike New York, I like this Philadelphia amazingly, and the people in it. There is only one thing that gets my "dander" up - and that is the hands are always encouraging me: telling me - "it's no use to get discouraged - no use to be down-hearted, for there is more work here than you can do!" "Down-hearted," the devil! I have not had a particle of such a feeling since I left Hannibal, more than four months ago. I fancy they'll have to wait some time till they see me down-hearted or afraid of starving while I have strength to work and am in a city of 400,000 inhabitants. When I was in Hannibal, before I had scarcely stepped out of the town limits, nothing could have convinced me that I would starve as soon as I got a little way from home....

The grave of Franklin is in Christ Church-yard, corner of Fifth and Arch streets. They keep the gates locked, and one can only see the flat slab that lies over his remains and that of his wife; but you cannot see the inscription distinctly enough to read it. The inscription, I believe, reads thus:

>"Benjamin |
>
>and | Franklin"
>
>Deborah |

I counted 27 cannons (6 pounders) planted in the edge of the sidewalk in Water St. the other day. They are driven into the ground, about a foot, with the mouth end upwards. A ball is driven fast into the mouth of each, to exclude the water; they look like so many posts. They were put there during the war. I have also seen them planted in this manner, round the old churches, in N. Y.....

There is one fine custom observed in Phila. A gentleman is always expected to hand up a lady's money for her. Yesterday, I sat in the front end of the 'bus, directly under the driver's box - a lady sat opposite me. She handed me her money, which was right. But, Lord! a St. Louis lady would think herself ruined, if she should be so familiar with a stranger. In St. Louis a man will sit in the front end of the stage, and see a lady stagger from the far end, to pay her fare. The Phila. 'bus drivers cannot cheat. In the front of the stage is a thing like an office clock, with figures from 0 to 40, marked on its face. When the stage starts, the hand of the clock is turned toward the 0. When you get in and pay your fare, the driver strikes a bell, and the hand moves to the figure 1 - that is, "one fare, and paid for," and there is your receipt, as good as if you had it in your pocket. When a passenger pays his fare and the driver does not strike the bell immediately, he is greeted "Strike that bell! will you?"

I must close now. I intend visiting the Navy Yard, Mint, etc., before I write again. You must write often. You see I have nothing to write interesting to you, while you can write nothing that will not interest me. Don't say my letters are not long enough. Tell Jim Wolfe to write. Tell all the boys where I am, and to write. Jim Robinson, particularly. I wrote to him from N. Y. Tell me all that is going on in H - l.

Truly your brother

SAM.

Those were primitive times. Imagine a passenger in these easy-going days calling to a driver or conductor to "Strike that bell!"

"H - l" is his abbreviation for Hannibal. He had first used it in a title of a poem which a few years before, during one of Orion's absences, he had published in the paper. "To Mary in Hannibal" was too long to set as a display head in single column. The poem had no great merit, but under the abbreviated title it could hardly fail to invite notice. It was one of several things he did to liven up the circulation during a brief period of his authority.

The doubtful money he mentions was the paper issued by private banks, "wild cat," as it was called. He had been paid with it in New York, and found it usually at a discount - sometimes even worthless. Wages and money were both better in Philadelphia, but the fund for his mother's trip to Kentucky apparently did not grow very rapidly.

The next letter, written a month later, is also to Orion Clemens, who had now moved to Muscatine, Iowa, and established there a new paper with an old title, 'The Journal'.

To Orion Clemens, in Muscatine, Iowa:

PHILADELPHIA, Nov. 28th, 1853.

MY DEAR BROTHER, - I received your letter today. I think Ma ought to spend the winter in St. Louis. I don't believe in that climate - it's too cold for her.

The printers' annual ball and supper came off the other night. The proceeds amounted to about $1,000. The printers, as well as other people, are endeavoring to raise money to erect a monument to Franklin, but there are so many abominable foreigners here (and among printers, too,) who hate everything American, that I am very certain as much money for such a purpose could be raised in St. Louis, as in Philadelphia. I was in Franklin's old office this morning - the "North American" (formerly "Philadelphia Gazette") and there was at least one foreigner for every American at work there.

How many subscribers has the Journal got? What does

the job-work pay? and what does the whole concern pay?.....

I will try to write for the paper occasionally, but I fear my letters will be very uninteresting, for this incessant night-work dulls one's ideas amazingly.

From some cause, I cannot set type nearly so fast as when I was at home. Sunday is a long day, and while others set 12 and 15,000, yesterday, I only set 10,000. However, I will shake this laziness off, soon, I reckon....

How do you like "free-soil?" - I would like amazingly to see a good old- fashioned negro.

My love to all

Truly your brother

SAM.

We may believe that it never occurred to the young printer, looking up landmarks of Ben Franklin, that time would show points of resemblance between the great Franklin's career and his own. Yet these seem now rather striking. Like Franklin, he had been taken out of school very young and put at the printer's trade; like Franklin, he had worked in his brother's office, and had written for the paper. Like him, too, he had left quietly for New York and Philadelphia to work at the trade of printing, and in time Samuel Clemens, like Benjamin Franklin, would become a world-figure, many-sided, human, and of incredible popularity. The boy Sam Clemens may have had such dreams, but we find no trace of them.

There is but one more letter of this early period. Young Clemens spent some time in Washington, but if he wrote from there his letters have disappeared. The last letter is from Philadelphia and seems to reflect homesickness. The novelty of absence and travel was wearing thin.

To Mrs. Moffett, in St. Louis:

PHILADELPHIA, Dec. 5, '53.

MY DEAR SISTER, - I have already written two letters within the last two hours, and you will excuse me if this is not lengthy. If I had the money, I would come to St. Louis now, while the river is open; but within the last two or three weeks I have spent about thirty dollars for clothing, so I suppose I shall remain where I am. I only want to return to avoid night-work, which is injuring my eyes. I have received one or two letters from home, but they are not written as they should be, and I know no more about what is going on there than the man in the moon. One only has to leave home to learn how to write an interesting letter to an absent friend when he gets back. I suppose you board at Mrs. Hunter's yet - and that, I think, is somewhere in Olive street above Fifth. Philadelphia is one of the healthiest places in the Union. I wanted to spend this winter in a warm climate, but it is too late now. I don't like our present prospect for cold weather at all.

Truly your brother

SAM.

But he did not return to the West for another half year. The letters he wrote during that period have not survived. It was late in the summer of 1854 when he finally started for St. Louis. He sat up for three days and nights in a smoking-car to make the journey, and arrived exhausted. The river packet was leaving in a few hours for Muscatine, Iowa, where his mother and his two brothers were now located. He paid his sister a brief visit, and caught the boat. Worn-out, he dropped into his berth and slept the thirty-six hours of the journey.

It was early when-he arrived - too early to arouse the family. In the office of the little hotel where he waited for daylight he found a small book. It contained portraits of the English rulers, with the brief facts of their reigns. Young Clemens entertained himself by learning this information by heart. He had a fine memory for such things, and in an hour or two had the printed data perfectly and permanently committed. This incidentally acquired knowledge proved of immense value to him. It was his groundwork for all English history.

II. LETTERS 1856-61.

KEOKUK, AND THE RIVER. END OF PILOTING

There comes a period now of nearly four years, when Samuel Clemens was either a poor correspondent or his letters have not been preserved. Only two from this time have survived - happily of intimate biographical importance.

Young Clemens had not remained in Muscatine. His brother had no inducements to offer, and he presently returned to St. Louis, where he worked as a compositor on the Evening News until the following spring, rooming with a young man named Burrough, a journeyman chair-maker with a taste for the English classics. Orion Clemens, meantime, on a trip to Keokuk, had casually married there, and a little later removed his office to that city. He did not move the paper; perhaps it did not seem worth while, and in Keokuk he confined himself to commercial printing. The Ben Franklin Book and Job Office started with fair prospects. Henry Clemens and a boy named Dick Hingham were the assistants, and somewhat later, when brother Sam came up from St. Louis on a visit, an offer of five dollars a week and board induced him to remain. Later, when it became increasingly difficult to pay the five dollars, Orion took his brother into partnership, which perhaps relieved the financial stress, though the office methods would seem to have left something to be desired. It is about at this point that the first of the two letters mentioned was written. The writer addressed it to his mother and sister - Jane Clemens having by this time taken up her home with her daughter, Mrs. Moffett.

To Mrs. Clemens and Mrs. Moffett, in St. Louis:

KEOKUK, Iowa, June 10th, 1856.

MY DEAR MOTHER & SISTER, - I have nothing to write. Everything is going on well. The Directory is coming on finely. I have to work on it occasionally, which I don't like a particle I don't like to work at too many things at once. They take Henry and Dick away from me too. Before we commenced the Directory, I could tell before breakfast just how much work could be done during the day, and manage accordingly - but now, they throw all my plans into disorder by taking my hands away from their work. I have nothing to do with the book - if I did I would have the two book hands do more work than they do, or else I would drop it. It is not a mere supposition that they do not work fast enough - I know it; for yesterday the two book hands were at work all day, Henry and Dick all the afternoon, on the advertisements, and they set up five pages and a half-and I set up two pages and a quarter of the same matter after supper, night before last, and I don't work fast on such things. They are either excessively slow motioned or very lazy. I am not getting along well with the job work. I can't work blindly - without system. I gave Dick a job yesterday, which I calculated he would set in two hours and I could work off in three, and therefore just finish it by supper time, but he was transferred to the Directory, and the job, promised this morning, remains untouched. Through all the great pressure of job work lately, I never before failed in a promise of the kind.

Your Son

    SAM

Excuse brevity this is my 3rd letter to-night.

Samuel Clemens was never celebrated for his patience; we may imagine that the disorder of the office tried his nerves. He seems, on the whole, however, to have been rather happy in Keokuk. There were plenty of young people there, and he was a favorite among them. But he had grown dissatisfied, and when one day some weeks later there fell into His hands an account of the riches of the newly explored regions of the upper Amazon, he promptly decided to find his fortune at the headwaters of the great South-American river. The second letter reports this momentous decision. It was written to Henry Clemens, who was temporarily absent-probably in Hannibal.

To Henry Clemens:

KEOKUK, August 5th, '56.

MY DEAR BROTHER, - ..... Ward and I held a long consultation, Sunday morning, and the result was that we two have determined to start to Brazil, if possible, in six weeks from now, in order to look carefully into matters there and report to Dr. Martin in time for him to follow on the first of March. We propose going via New York. Now, between you and I and the fence you must say nothing about this to Orion, for he thinks that Ward is to go clear through alone, and that I am to stop at New York or New Orleans until he reports. But that don't suit me. My confidence in human nature does not extend quite that far. I won't depend upon Ward's judgment, or anybody's else - I want to see with my own eyes, and form my own opinion. But you know what Orion is. When he gets a notion into his head, and more especially if it is an erroneous one, the Devil can't get it out again. So I know better than to combat his arguments long, but apparently yielded, inwardly determined to go clear through. Ma knows my determination, but even she counsels me to keep it from Orion. She says I can treat him as I did her when I started to St. Louis and went to New York - I can start to New York and go to South America! Although Orion talks grandly about furnishing me with fifty or a hundred dollars in six weeks, I could not depend upon him for ten dollars, so I have "feelers" out in several directions, and have already asked for a hundred dollars from one source (keep it to yourself.) I will lay on my oars for awhile, and see how the wind sets, when I may probably try to get more. Mrs. Creel is a great friend of mine, and has some influence with Ma and Orion, though I reckon they would not acknowledge it. I am going up there tomorrow, to press her into my service. I shall take care that Ma and Orion are plentifully supplied with South American books. They have Herndon's Report now. Ward and the Dr. and myself will hold a grand consultation tonight at the office. We have agreed that no more shall be admitted into our company.

I believe the Guards went down to Quincy today to escort our first locomotive home.

Write soon.

Your Brother,

SAM.

Readers familiar with the life of Mark Twain know that none of the would-be adventurers found their way to the Amazon: His two associates gave up the plan, probably for lack of means. Young Clemens himself found a fifty-dollar bill one bleak November day blowing along the streets of Keokuk, and after duly advertising his find without result, set out for the Amazon, by way of Cincinnati and New Orleans.

"I advertised the find and left for the Amazon the same day," he once declared, a statement which we may take with a literary discount.

He remained in Cincinnati that winter (1856-57) working at his trade. No letters have been preserved from that time, except two that were sent to a Keokuk weekly, the Saturday Post, and as these were written for publication, and are rather a poor attempt at burlesque humor - their chief feature being a pretended illiteracy - they would seem to bear no relation to this collection. He roomed that winter with a rugged, self-educated Scotchman - a mechanic, but a man of books and philosophies, who left an impress on Mark Twain's mental life.

In April he took up once more the journey toward South America, but presently forgot the Amazon altogether in the new career that opened to him. All through his boyhood and youth Samuel Clemens had wanted to be a pilot. Now came the long-deferred opportunity. On the little Cincinnati steamer, the Paul Jones, there was a pilot named Horace Bixby. Young Clemens idling in the pilot-house was one morning seized with the old ambition, and laid siege to Bixby to teach him the river. The terms finally agreed upon specified a fee to Bixby of five hundred dollars, one hundred down, the balance when the pupil had completed the course and was earning money. But all this has been told in full elsewhere, and is only summarized here because the letters fail to complete the story.

Bixby soon made some trips up the Missouri River, and in his absence turned his apprentice, or "cub," over to other pilots, such being the river custom. Young Clemens, in love with the life, and a favorite with his superiors, had a happy time until he came under a pilot named Brown. Brown was illiterate and tyrannical, and from the beginning of their association pilot and apprentice disliked each other cordially.

It is at this point that the letters begin once more - the first having been written when young Clemens, now twenty-two years old, had been on the river nearly a year. Life with Brown, of course, was not all sorrow and in this letter we find some of the fierce joy of adventure which in those days Samuel Clemens loved.

To Onion Clemens and Wife, in Keokuk, Iowa:

SAINT LOUIS, March 9th, 1858.

DEAR BROTHER AND SISTER, - I must take advantage of the opportunity now presented to write you, but I shall necessarily be dull, as I feel uncommonly stupid. We have had a hard trip this time. Left Saint Louis three weeks ago on the Pennsylvania. The weather was very cold, and the ice running densely. We got 15 miles below town, landed the boat, and then one pilot. Second Mate and four deck hands took the sounding boat and shoved out in the ice to hunt the channel. They failed to find it, and the ice drifted them ashore. The pilot left the men with the boat and walked back to us, a mile and a half. Then the other pilot and myself, with a larger crew of men started out and met with the same fate. We drifted ashore just below the other boat. Then the fun commenced. We made fast a line 20 fathoms long, to the bow of the yawl, and put the men (both crews) to it like horses, on the shore. Brown, the pilot, stood in the bow, with an oar, to keep her head out, and I took the tiller. We would start the men, and all would go well till the yawl would bring up on a heavy cake of ice, and then the men would drop like so many ten-pins, while Brown assumed the horizontal in the bottom of the boat. After an hour's hard work we got back, with ice half an inch thick on the oars. Sent back and warped up the other yawl, and then George (the first mentioned pilot,) and myself, took a double crew of fresh men and tried it again. This time we found the channel in less than half an hour, and landed on an island till the Pennsylvania came along and took us off. The next day was colder still. I was out in the yawl twice, and then we got through, but the infernal steamboat came near running over us. We went ten miles further, landed, and George and I cleared out again - found the channel first trial, but got caught in the gorge and drifted helplessly down the river. The Ocean Spray came along and started into the ice after us, but although she didn't succeed in her kind intention of taking us aboard, her waves washed us out, and that was all we wanted. We landed on an island, built a big fire and waited for the boat. She started, and ran aground! It commenced raining and sleeting, and a very interesting time we had on that barren sandbar for the next four hours, when the boat got off and took us aboard. The next day was terribly cold. We sounded Hat Island, warped up around a bar and sounded again - but in order to understand our situation you will have to read Dr. Kane. It would have been impossible to get back to the boat. But the Maria Denning was aground at the head of the island - they hailed us - we ran alongside and they hoisted us in and thawed us out. We had then been out in the yawl from 4 o'clock in the morning till half past 9 without being near a fire. There was a thick coating of ice over men, yawl, ropes and everything else, and we looked like rock-candy statuary. We got to Saint Louis this morning, after an absence of 3 weeks - that boat generally makes the trip in 2.

Henry was doing little or nothing here, and I sent him to our clerk to work his way for a trip, by measuring wood piles, counting coal boxes, and other clerkly duties, which he performed satisfactorily. He may go down with us again, for I expect he likes our bill of fare better than that of his boarding house.

I got your letter at Memphis as I went down. That is the best place to write me at. The post office here is always out of my route, somehow or other. Remember the direction: "S.L.C., Steamer Pennsylvania Care Duval & Algeo, Wharfboat, Memphis." I cannot correspond with a paper, because when one is learning the river, he is not allowed to do or think about anything else.

I am glad to see you in such high spirits about the land, and I hope you will remain so, if you never get richer. I seldom venture to think about our landed wealth, for "hope deferred maketh the heart sick."

I did intend to answer your letter, but I am too lazy and too sleepy now. We have had a rough time during the last 24 hours working through the ice between Cairo and Saint Louis, and I have had but little rest.

I got here too late to see the funeral of the 10 victims by the burning of the Pacific hotel in 7th street. Ma says there were 10 hearses, with the fire companies (their engines in mourning - firemen in uniform,) the various benevolent societies in uniform and mourning, and a multitude of citizens and strangers, forming, altogether, a procession of 30,000 persons! One steam fire engine was drawn by four white horses, with crape festoons on their heads.

Well I am - just - about - asleep -

Your brother

SAM.

Among other things, we gather from this letter that Orion Clemens had faith in his brother as a newspaper correspondent, though the two contributions from Cincinnati, already mentioned, were not promising. Furthermore, we get an intimation of Orion's unfailing confidence in the future of the "land" - that is to say, the great tract of land in Eastern Tennessee which, in an earlier day, his father had bought as a heritage for his children. It is the same Tennessee land that had "millions in it" for Colonel Sellers - the land that would become, as Orion Clemens long afterward phrased it, "the worry of three generations."

The Doctor Kane of this letter is, of course, Dr. Elisha Kent Kane, the American Arctic explorer. Any book of exploration always appealed to Mark Twain, and in those days Kane was a favorite.

The paragraph concerning Henry, and his employment on the Pennsylvania, begins the story of a tragedy. The story has been fully told elsewhere, - [Mark Twain: A Biography, by same author.] - and need only be sketched briefly here. Henry, a gentle, faithful boy, shared with his brother the enmity of the pilot Brown. Some two months following the date of the foregoing letter, on a down trip of the Pennsylvania, an unprovoked attack made by Brown upon the boy brought his brother Sam to the rescue. Brown received a good pummeling at the hands of the future humorist, who, though upheld by the captain, decided to quit the Pennsylvania at New Orleans and to come up the river by another boat. The Brown episode has no special bearing on the main tragedy, though now in retrospect it seems closely related to it. Samuel Clemens, coming up the river on the A. T. Lacey, two days behind the Pennsylvania, heard a voice shout as they approached the Greenville, Mississippi, landing:

"The Pennsylvania is blown up just below Memphis, at Ship Island! One hundred and fifty lives lost!"

It was a true report. At six o'clock of a warm, mid-June morning, while loading wood, sixty miles below Memphis, the Pennsylvania's boilers had exploded with fearful results. Henry Clemens was among the injured. He was still alive when his brother reached Memphis on the Lacey, but died a few days later. Samuel Clemens had idolized the boy, and regarded himself responsible for his death. The letter that follows shows that he was overwrought by the scenes about him and the strain of watching, yet the anguish of it is none the less real.

To Mrs. Onion Clemens:

DEAR SISTER MOLLIE, - Long before this reaches you, my poor Henry my darling, my pride, my glory, my all, will have finished his blameless career, and the light of my life will have gone out in utter darkness. (O, God! this is hard to bear.) Hardened, hopeless, - aye, lost - lost - lost and ruined sinner as I am - I, even I, have humbled myself to the ground and prayed as never man prayed before, that the great God might let this cup pass from me - that he would strike me to the earth, but spare my brother - that he would pour out the fulness of his just wrath upon my wicked head, but have mercy, mercy, mercy upon that unoffending boy. The horrors of three days have swept over me - they have blasted my youth and left me an old man before my time. Mollie, there are gray hairs in my head tonight. For forty-eight hours I labored at the bedside of my poor burned and bruised, but uncomplaining brother, and then the star of my hope went out and left me in the gloom of despair. Men take me by the hand and congratulate me, and call me "lucky" because I was not on the Pennsylvania when she blew up! May God forgive them, for they know not what they say.

Mollie you do not understand why I was not on that boat - I will tell you. I left Saint Louis on her, but on the way down, Mr. Brown, the pilot that was killed by the explosion (poor fellow,) quarreled with Henry without cause, while I was steering. Henry started out of the pilot-house - Brown jumped up and collared him - turned him half way around and struck him in the face! - and him nearly six feet high - struck my little brother. I was wild from that moment. I left the boat to steer herself, and avenged the insult - and the Captain said I was right - that he would discharge Brown in N. Orleans if he could get another pilot, and would do it in St. Louis, anyhow. Of course both of us could not return to St. Louis on the same boat - no pilot could be found, and the Captain sent me to the A. T. Lacey, with orders to her Captain to bring me to Saint Louis. Had another pilot been found, poor Brown would have been the "lucky" man.

I was on the Pennsylvania five minutes before she left N. Orleans, and I must tell you the truth, Mollie - three hundred human beings perished by that fearful disaster. Henry was asleep - was blown up - then fell back on the hot boilers, and I suppose that rubbish fell on him, for he is injured internally. He got into the water and swam to shore, and got into the flatboat with the other survivors. - [Henry had returned once to the Pennsylvania to render assistance to the passengers. Later he had somehow made his way to the flatboat.] - He had nothing on but his wet shirt, and he lay there burning up with a southern sun and freezing in the wind till the Kate Frisbee came along. His wounds were not dressed till he got to Memphis, 15 hours after the explosion. He was senseless and motionless for 12 hours after that. But may God bless Memphis, the noblest city on the face of the earth. She has done her duty by these poor afflicted creatures - especially Henry, for he has had five - aye, ten, fifteen, twenty times the care and attention that any one else has had. Dr. Peyton, the best physician in Memphis (he is exactly like the portraits of Webster) sat by him for 36 hours. There are 32 scalded men in that room, and you would know Dr. Peyton better than I can describe him, if you could follow him around and hear each man murmur as he passes, "May the God of Heaven bless you, Doctor!" The ladies have done well, too. Our second Mate, a handsome, noble hearted young fellow, will die. Yesterday a beautiful girl of 15 stooped timidly down by his side and handed him a pretty bouquet. The poor suffering boy's eyes kindled, his lips quivered out a gentle "God bless you, Miss," and he burst into tears. He made them write her name on a card for him, that he might not forget it.

Pray for me, Mollie, and pray for my poor sinless brother.

Your unfortunate Brother,

SAML. L. CLEMENS.

P. S. I got here two days after Henry.

It is said that Mark Twain never really recovered from the tragedy of his brother's death - that it was responsible for the serious, pathetic look that the face of the world's greatest laugh-maker always wore in repose.

He went back to the river, and in September of the same year, after an apprenticeship of less than eighteen months, received his license as a St. Louis and New Orleans pilot, and was accepted by his old chief, Bixby, as full partner on an important boat. In Life on the Mississippi Mark Twain makes the period of his study from two to two and a half years, but this is merely an attempt to magnify his dullness. He was, in fact, an apt pupil and a pilot of very high class.

Clemens was now suddenly lifted to a position of importance. The Mississippi River pilot of those days was a person of distinction, earning a salary then regarded as princely. Certainly two hundred and fifty dollars a month was large for a boy of twenty-three. At once, of course, he became the head of the Clemens family. His brother Orion was ten years older, but he had not the gift of success. By common consent the younger brother assumed permanently the position of family counselor and financier. We expect him to feel the importance of his new position, and he is too human to disappoint us. Incidentally, we notice an improvement in his English. He no longer writes "between you and I"

Fragment of a letter to Orion Clemens. Written at St. Louis in 1859:

.....I am not talking nonsense, now - I am in earnest, I want you to keep your troubles and your plans out of the reach of meddlers, until the latter are consummated, so that in case you fail, no one will know it but yourself.

Above all things (between you and me) never tell Ma any of your troubles; she never slept a wink the night your last letter came, and she looks distressed yet. Write only cheerful news to her. You know that she will not be satisfied so long as she thinks anything is going on that she is ignorant of - and she makes a little fuss about it when her suspicions are awakened; but that makes no difference - . I know that it is better that she be kept in the dark concerning all things of an unpleasant nature. She upbraids me occasionally for giving her only the bright side of my affairs (but unfortunately for her she has to put up with it, for I know that troubles that I curse awhile and forget, would disturb her slumbers for some time.) (Parenthesis No. 2 - Possibly because she is deprived of the soothing consolation of swearing.) Tell her the good news and me the bad.

Putting all things together, I begin to think I am rather lucky than otherwise - a notion which I was slow to take up. The other night I was about to round to for a storm - but concluded that I could find a smoother bank somewhere. I landed 5 miles below. The storm came - passed away and did not injure us. Coming up, day before yesterday, I looked at the spot I first chose, and half the trees on the bank were torn to shreds. We couldn't have lived 5 minutes in such a tornado. And I am also lucky in having a berth, while all the young pilots are idle. This is the luckiest circumstance that ever befell me. Not on account of the wages - for that is a secondary consideration - but from the fact that the City of Memphis is the largest boat in the trade and the hardest to pilot, and consequently I can get a reputation on her, which is a thing I never could accomplish on a transient boat. I can "bank" in the neighborhood of $100 a month on her, and that will satisfy me for the present (principally because the other youngsters are sucking their fingers.) Bless me! what a pleasure there is in revenge! and what vast respect Prosperity commands! Why, six months ago, I could enter the "Rooms," and receive only a customary fraternal greeting - but now they say, "Why, how are you, old fellow - when did you get in?"

And the young pilots who used to tell me, patronizingly, that I could never learn the river cannot keep from showing a little of their chagrin at seeing me so far ahead of them. Permit me to "blow my horn," for I derive a living pleasure from these things, and I must confess that when I go to pay my dues, I rather like to let the d - d rascals get a glimpse of a hundred dollar bill peeping out from amongst notes of smaller dimensions, whose face I do not exhibit! You will despise this egotism, but I tell you there is a "stern joy" in it.....

Pilots did not remain long on one boat, as a rule; just why it is not so easy to understand. Perhaps they liked the experience of change; perhaps both captain and pilot liked the pursuit of the ideal. In the light-hearted letter that follows - written to a friend of the family, formerly of Hannibal - we get something of the uncertainty of the pilot's engagements.

To Mrs. Elizabeth W. Smith, in Jackson, Cape Girardeau County, Mo.:

ST. Louis, Oct. 31 [probably 1859].

DEAR AUNT BETSEY, - Ma has not written you, because she did not know when I would get started down the river again.....

You see, Aunt Betsey, I made but one trip on the packet after you left, and then concluded to remain at home awhile. I have just discovered this morning that I am to go to New Orleans on the "Col. Chambers" - fine, light-draught, swift-running passenger steamer - all modern accommodations and improvements - through with dispatch - for freight or passage apply on board, or to - but - I have forgotten the agent's name - however, it makes no difference - and as I was saying, or had intended to say, Aunt Betsey, probably, if you are ready to come up, you had better take the "Ben Lewis," the best boat in the packet line. She will be at Cape Girardeau at noon on Saturday (day after tomorrow,) and will reach here at breakfast time, Sunday. If Mr. Hamilton is chief clerk, - very well, I am slightly acquainted with him. And if Messrs. Carter Gray and Dean Somebody (I have forgotten his other name,) are in the pilot-house - very well again-I am acquainted with them. Just tell Mr. Gray, Aunt Betsey - that I wish him to place himself at your command.

All the family are well - except myself - I am in a bad way again - disease, Love, in its most malignant form. Hopes are entertained of my recovery, however. At the dinner table - excellent symptom - I am still as "terrible as an army with banners."

Aunt Betsey - the wickedness of this world - but I haven't time to moralize this morning.

Goodbye

SAM CLEMENS.

As we do not hear of this "attack" again, the recovery was probably prompt. His letters are not frequent enough for us to keep track of his boats, but we know that he was associated with Bixby from time to time, and now and again with one of the Bowen boys, his old Hannibal schoolmates. He was reveling in the river life, the ease and distinction and romance of it. No other life would ever suit him as well. He was at the age to enjoy just what it brought him - at the airy, golden, overweening age of youth.

To Orion Clemens, in Keokuk, Iowa:

ST. LOUIS, Mch. 1860.

MY DEAR BRO., - Your last has just come to hand. It reminds me strongly of Tom Hood's letters to his family, (which I have been reading lately). But yours only remind me of his, for although there is a striking likeness, your humour is much finer than his, and far better expressed. Tom Hood's wit, (in his letters) has a savor of labor about it which is very disagreeable. Your letter is good. That portion of it wherein the old sow figures is the very best thing I have seen lately. Its quiet style resembles Goldsmith's "Citizen of the World," and "Don Quixote," - which are my beau ideals of fine writing.

You have paid the preacher! Well, that is good, also. What a man wants with religion in these breadless times, surpasses my comprehension.

Pamela and I have just returned from a visit to the most wonderfully beautiful painting which this city has ever seen - Church's "Heart of the Andes" - which represents a lovely valley with its rich vegetation in all the bloom and glory of a tropical summer - dotted with birds and flowers of all colors and shades of color, and sunny slopes, and shady corners, and twilight groves, and cool cascades - all grandly set off with a majestic mountain in the background with its gleaming summit clothed in everlasting ice and snow! I have seen it several times, but it is always a new picture - totally new - you seem to see nothing the second time which you saw the first. We took the opera glass, and examined its beauties minutely, for the naked eye cannot discern the little wayside flowers, and soft shadows and patches of sunshine, and half-hidden bunches of grass and jets of water which form some of its most enchanting features. There is no slurring of perspective effect about it - the most distant - the minutest object in it has a marked and distinct personality - so that you may count the very leaves on the trees. When you first see the tame, ordinary-looking picture, your first impulse is to turn your back upon it, and say "Humbug" - but your third visit will find your brain gasping and straining with futile efforts to take all the wonder in - and appreciate it in its fulness - and understand how such a miracle could have been conceived and executed by human brain and human hands. You will never get tired of looking at the picture, but your reflections - your efforts to grasp an intelligible Something - you hardly know what - will grow so painful that you will have to go away from the thing, in order to obtain relief. You may find relief, but you cannot banish the picture - It remains with you still. It is in my mind now - and the smallest feature could not be removed without my detecting it. So much for the "Heart of the Andes."

Ma was delighted with her trip, but she was disgusted with the girls for allowing me to embrace and kiss them - and she was horrified at the Schottische as performed by Miss Castle and myself. She was perfectly willing for me to dance until 12 o'clock at the imminent peril of my going to sleep on the after watch - but then she would top off with a very inconsistent sermon on dancing in general; ending with a terrific broadside aimed at that heresy of heresies, the Schottische.

I took Ma and the girls in a carriage, round that portion of New Orleans where the finest gardens and residences are to be seen, and although it was a blazing hot dusty day, they seemed hugely delighted. To use an expression which is commonly ignored in polite society, they were "hell-bent" on stealing some of the luscious-looking oranges from branches which overhung the fences, but I restrained them. They were not aware before that shrubbery could be made to take any queer shape which a skilful gardener might choose to twist it into, so they found not only beauty but novelty in their visit. We went out to Lake Pontchartrain in the cars.

Your Brother

SAM CLEMENS

We have not before heard of Miss Castle, who appears to have been one of the girls who accompanied Jane Clemens on the trip which her son gave her to New Orleans, but we may guess that the other was his cousin and good comrade, Ella Creel. One wishes that he might have left us a more extended account of that long-ago river journey, a fuller glimpse of a golden age that has vanished as completely as the days of Washington.

We may smile at the natural youthful desire to air his reading, and his art appreciation, and we may find his opinions not without interest. We may even commend them - in part. Perhaps we no longer count the leaves on Church's trees, but Goldsmith and Cervantes still deserve the place assigned them.

He does not tell us what boat he was on at this time, but later in the year he was with Bixby again, on the Alonzo Child. We get a bit of the pilot in port in his next.

To Orion Clemens, in Keokuk, Iowa:

"ALONZO CHILD," N. ORLEANS, Sep. 28th 1860.

DEAR BROTHER, - I just received yours and Mollies letter yesterday -they ad been here two weeks - forwarded from St. Louis. We got here esterday - will leave at noon to-day. Of course I have had no time, in 24 hours, to do anything. Therefore I'll answer after we are under way again. Yesterday, I had many things to do, but Bixby and I got with the pilots of two other boats and went off dissipating on a ten dollar dinner at a French restaurant breathe it not unto Ma! - where we ate sheep-head, fish with mushrooms, shrimps and oysters - birds - coffee with brandy burnt in it, &c &c,- ate, drank and smoked, from 2 p.m. until 5 o'clock, and then - then the day was too far gone to do any thing.

Please find enclosed and acknowledge receipt of - $20.00

In haste

SAM L. CLEMENS

It should be said, perhaps, that when he became pilot Jane Clemens had released her son from his pledge in the matter of cards and liquor. This license did not upset him, however. He cared very little for either of these dissipations. His one great indulgence was tobacco, a matter upon which he was presently to receive some grave counsel. He reports it in his next letter, a sufficiently interesting document. The clairvoyant of this visit was Madame Caprell, famous in her day. Clemens had been urged to consult her, and one idle afternoon concluded to make the experiment. The letter reporting the matter to his brother is fragmentary, and is the last remaining to us of the piloting period.

Fragment of a letter to Orion Clemens, in Keokuk, Iowa:

NEW ORLEANS February 6, 1862.

.....She's a very pleasant little lady - rather pretty - about 28, - say 5 feet 2 and one quarter - would weigh 116 - has black eyes and hair - is polite and intelligent - used good language, and talks much faster than I do.

She invited me into the little back parlor, closed the door; and we were alone. We sat down facing each other. Then she asked my age. Then she put her hands before her eyes a moment, and commenced talking as if she had a good deal to say and not much time to say it in. Something after this style:

MADAME. Yours is a watery planet; you gain your livelihood on the water; but you should have been a lawyer - there is where your talents lie: you might have distinguished yourself as an orator, or as an editor; you have written a great deal; you write well - but you are rather out of practice; no matter - you will be in practice some day; you have a superb constitution, and as excellent health as any man in the world; you have great powers of endurance; in your profession your strength holds out against the longest sieges, without flagging; still, the upper part of your lungs, the top of them is slightly affected - you must take care of yourself; you do not drink, but you use entirely too much tobacco; and you must stop it; mind, not moderate, but stop the use of it totally; then I can almost promise you 86 when you will surely die; otherwise look out for 28, 31, 34, 47, and 65; be careful - for you are not of a long-lived race, that is on your father's side; you are the only healthy member of your family, and the only one in it who has anything like the certainty of attaining to a great age - so, stop using tobacco, and be careful of yourself..... In some respects you take after your father, but you are much more like your mother, who belongs to the long-lived, energetic side of the house.... You never brought all your energies to bear upon any subject but what you accomplished it - for instance, you are self-made, self-educated.

S. L. C. Which proves nothing.

MADAME. Don't interrupt. When you sought your present occupation you found a thousand obstacles in the way - obstacles unknown - not even suspected by any save you and me, since you keep such matters to yourself - but you fought your way, and hid the long struggle under a mask of cheerfulness, which saved your friends anxiety on your account. To do
all this requires all the qualities I have named.

S. L. C. You flatter well, Madame.

MADAME. Don't interrupt: Up to within a short time you had always lived from hand to mouth-now you are in easy circumstances - for which you need give credit to no one but yourself. The turning point in your life occurred in 1840-7-8.

S. L. C. Which was?

MADAME. A death perhaps, and this threw you upon the world and made you what you are; it was always intended that you should make yourself; therefore, it was well that this calamity occurred as early as it did. You will never die of water, although your career upon it in the future seems well sprinkled with misfortune. You will continue upon the water for some time yet; you will not retire finally until ten years from now .... What is your brother's age? 35 - and a lawyer? and in pursuit of an office? Well, he stands a better chance than the other two, and he may get it; he is too visionary - is always flying off on a new hobby; this will never do - tell him I said so. He is a good lawyer - a, very good lawyer - and a fine speaker - is very popular and much respected, and makes many friends; but although he retains their friendship, he loses their confidence by displaying his instability of character..... The land he has now will be very valuable after a while -

S. L. C. Say a 50 years hence, or thereabouts. Madame -

MADAME. No - less time-but never mind the land, that is a secondary consideration - let him drop that for the present, and devote himself to his business and politics with all his might, for he must hold offices under the Government.....

After a while you will possess a good deal of property - retire at the end of ten years - after which your pursuits will be literary - try the law - you will certainly succeed. I am done now. If you have any questions to ask - ask them freely - and if it be in my power, I will answer without reserve - without reserve.

I asked a few questions of minor importance - paid her $2 - and left, under the decided impression that going to the fortune teller's was just as good as going to the opera, and the cost scarcely a trifle more - ergo, I will disguise myself and go again, one of these days, when other amusements fail. Now isn't she the devil? That is to say, isn't she a right smart little woman?

When you want money, let Ma know, and she will send it. She and Pamela are always fussing about change, so I sent them a hundred and twenty quarters yesterday - fiddler's change enough to last till I get back, I reckon.

SAM.

It is not so difficult to credit Madame Caprell with clairvoyant powers when one has read the letters of Samuel Clemens up to this point. If we may judge by those that have survived, her prophecy of literary distinction for him was hardly warranted by anything she could have known of his past performance. These letters of his youth have a value to-day only because they were written by the man who later was to become Mark Twain. The squibs and skits which he sometimes contributed to the New Orleans papers were bright, perhaps, and pleasing to his pilot associates, but they were without literary value. He was twenty-five years old. More than one author has achieved reputation at that age. Mark Twain was of slower growth; at that age he had not even developed a definite literary ambition: Whatever the basis of Madame Caprell's prophecy, we must admit that she was a good guesser on several matters, "a right smart little woman," as Clemens himself phrased it.

She overlooked one item, however: the proximity of the Civil War. Perhaps it was too close at hand for second sight. A little more than two months after the Caprell letter was written Fort Sumter was fired upon. Mask Twain had made his last trip as a pilot up the river to St. Louis - the nation was plunged into a four years' conflict.

There are no letters of this immediate period. Young Clemens went to Hannibal, and enlisting in a private company, composed mainly of old schoolmates, went soldiering for two rainy, inglorious weeks, by the end of which he had had enough of war, and furthermore had discovered that he was more of a Union abolitionist than a slave-holding secessionist, as he had at first supposed. Convictions were likely to be rather infirm during those early days of the war, and subject to change without notice. Especially was this so in a border State.

III. LETTERS 1861-62.

ON THE FRONTIER. MINING ADVENTURES. JOURNALISTIC BEGINNINGS

Clemens went from the battle-front to Keokuk, where Orion was preparing to accept the appointment prophesied by Madame Caprell. Orion was a stanch Unionist, and a member of Lincoln's Cabinet had offered him the secretaryship of the new Territory of Nevada. Orion had accepted, and only needed funds to carry him to his destination. His pilot brother had the funds, and upon being appointed "private" secretary, agreed to pay both passages on the overland stage, which would bear them across the great plains from St. Jo to Carson City. Mark Twain, in Roughing It, has described that glorious journey and the frontier life that followed it. His letters form a supplement of realism to a tale that is more or less fictitious, though marvelously true in color and background. The first bears no date, but it was written not long after their arrival, August 14, 1861. It is not complete, but there is enough of it to give us a very fair picture of Carson City, "a wooden town; its population two thousand souls."

Part of a letter to Mrs. Jane Clemens, in St. Louis:

(Date not given, but Sept, or Oct., 1861.)

MY DEAR MOTHER, - I hope you will all come out here someday. But I shan't consent to invite you, until we can receive you in style. But I guess we shall be able to do that, one of these days. I intend that Pamela shall live on Lake Bigler until she can knock a bull down with her fist - say, about three months.

"Tell everything as it is - no better, and no worse."

Well, "Gold Hill" sells at $5,000 per foot, cash down; "Wild cat" isn't worth ten cents. The country is fabulously rich in gold, silver, copper, lead, coal, iron, quick silver, marble, granite, chalk, plaster of Paris, (gypsum,) thieves, murderers, desperadoes, ladies, children, lawyers, Christians, Indians, Chinamen, Spaniards, gamblers, sharpers, coyotes (pronounced Ki-yo-ties,) poets, preachers, and jackass rabbits. I overheard a gentleman say, the other day, that it was "the d - dest country under the sun." - and that comprehensive conception I fully subscribe to. It never rains here, and the dew never falls. No flowers grow here, and no green thing gladdens the eye. The birds that fly over the land carry their provisions with them. Only the crow and the raven tarry with us. Our city lies in the midst of a desert of the purest - most unadulterated, and compromising sand - in which infernal soil nothing but that fag-end of vegetable creation, "sage-brush," ventures to grow. If you will take a Lilliputian cedar tree for a model, and build a dozen imitations of it with the stiffest article of telegraph wire - set them one foot apart and then try to walk through them, you'll understand (provided the floor is covered 12 inches deep with sand,) what it is to wander through a sage-brush desert. When crushed, sage brush emits an odor which isn't exactly magnolia and equally isn't exactly polecat but is a sort of compromise between the two. It looks a good deal like grease-wood, and is the ugliest plant that was ever conceived of. It is gray in color. On the plains, sage-brush and grease-wood grow about twice as large as the common geranium - and in my opinion they are a very good substitute for that useless vegetable. Grease-wood is a perfect-most perfect imitation in miniature of a live oak tree-barring the color of it. As to the other fruits and flowers of the country, there ain't any, except "Pulu" or "Tuler," or what ever they call it, - a species of unpoetical willow that grows on the banks of the Carson - a RIVER, 20 yards wide, knee deep, and so villainously rapid and crooked, that it looks like it had wandered into the country without intending it, and had run about in a bewildered way and got lost, in its hurry to get out again before some thirsty man came along and drank it up. I said we are situated in a flat, sandy desert - true. And surrounded on all sides by such prodigious mountains, that when you gaze at them awhile, - and begin to conceive of their grandeur - and next to feel their vastness expanding your soul - and ultimately find yourself growing and swelling and spreading into a giant - I say when this point is reached, you look disdainfully down upon the insignificant village of Carson, and in that instant you are seized with a burning desire to stretch forth your hand, put the city in your pocket, and walk off with it.

As to churches, I believe they have got a Catholic one here, but like that one the New York fireman spoke of,

I believe "they don't run her now:" Now, although we are surrounded by sand, the greatest part of the town is built upon what was once a very pretty grassy spot; and the streams of pure water that used to poke about it in rural sloth and solitude, now pass through on dusty streets and gladden the hearts of men by reminding them that there is at least something here that hath its prototype among the homes they left behind them. And up "King's Canon," (please pronounce canyon, after the manner of the natives,) there are "ranches," or farms, where they say hay grows, and grass, and beets and onions, and turnips, and other "truck" which is suitable for cows - yes, and even Irish potatoes; also, cabbage, peas and beans.

The houses are mostly frame, unplastered, but "papered" inside with flour-sacks sewed together, and the handsomer the "brand" upon the sacks is, the neater the house looks. Occasionally, you stumble on a stone house. On account of the dryness of the country, the shingles on the houses warp till they look like short joints of stove pipe split lengthwise.

(Remainder missing.)

In this letter is something of the "wild freedom of the West," which later would contribute to his fame. The spirit of the frontier - of Mark Twain - was beginning to stir him.

There had been no secretary work for him to do, and no provision for payment. He found his profit in studying human nature and in prospecting native resources. He was not interested in mining not yet. With a boy named John Kinney he made an excursion to Lake Bigler - now Tahoe - and located a timber claim, really of great value. They were supposed to build a fence around it, but they were too full of the enjoyment of camp-life to complete it. They put in most of their time wandering through the stately forest or drifting over the transparent lake in a boat left there by lumbermen. They built themselves a brush house, but they did not sleep in it. In 'Roughing It' he writes, "It never occurred to us, for one thing; and, besides, it was built to hold the ground, and that was enough. We did not wish to strain it."

They were having a glorious time, when their camp-fire got away from them and burned up their claim. His next letter, of which the beginning is missing, describes the fire.

Fragment of a letter to Mrs. Jane Clemens and Mrs. Moffett, in St. Louis:

.....The level ranks of flame were relieved at intervals by the standard-bearers, as we called the tall dead trees, wrapped in fire, and waving their blazing banners a hundred feet in the air. Then we could turn from this scene to the Lake, and see every branch, and leaf, and cataract of flame upon its bank perfectly reflected as in a gleaming, fiery mirror. The mighty roaring of the conflagration, together with our solitary and somewhat unsafe position (for there was no one within six miles of us,) rendered the scene very impressive. Occasionally, one of us would remove his pipe from his mouth and say, "Superb! magnificent! Beautiful! but-by the Lord God Almighty, if we attempt to sleep in this little patch tonight, we'll never live till morning! for if we don't burn up, we'll certainly suffocate." But he was persuaded to sit up until we felt pretty safe as far as the fire was concerned, and then we turned in, with many misgivings. When we got up in the morning, we found that the fire had burned small pieces of drift wood within six feet of our boat, and had made its way to within 4 or 5 steps of us on the South side. We looked like lava men, covered as we were with ashes, and begrimed with smoke. We were very black in the face, but we soon washed ourselves white again.

John D. Kinney, a Cincinnati boy, and a first-rate fellow, too, who came out with judge Turner, was my comrade. We staid at the Lake four days - I had plenty of fun, for John constantly reminded me of Sam Bowen when we were on our campaign in Missouri. But first and foremost, for Annie's, Mollies, and Pamela's comfort, be it known that I have never been guilty of profane language since I have been in this Territory, and Kinney hardly ever swears. - But sometimes human nature gets the better of him. On the second day we started to go by land to the lower camp, a distance of three miles, over the mountains, each carrying an axe. I don't think we got lost exactly, but we wandered four hours over the steepest, rockiest and most dangerous piece of country in the world. I couldn't keep from laughing at Kinney's distress, so I kept behind, so that he could not see me. After he would get over a dangerous place, with infinite labor and constant apprehension, he would stop, lean on his axe, and look around, then behind, then ahead, and then drop his head and ruminate awhile. - Then he would draw a long sigh, and say: "Well - could any Billygoat have scaled that place without breaking his - ---- neck?" And I would reply, "No, - I don't think he could." "No - you don't think he could - " (mimicking me,) "Why don't you curse the infernal place? You know you want to. - I do, and will curse the ----- thieving country as long as I live." Then we would toil on in silence for awhile. Finally I told him - "Well, John, what if we don't find our way out of this today - we'll know all about the country when we do get out." "Oh stuff - I know enough - and too much about the d - -d villainous locality already." Finally, we reached the camp. But as we brought no provisions with us, the first subject that presented itself to us was, how to get back. John swore he wouldn't walk back, so we rolled a drift log apiece into the Lake, and set about making paddles, intending to straddle the logs and paddle ourselves back home sometime or other. But the Lake objected - got stormy, and we had to give it up. So we set out for the only house on this side of the Lake - three miles from there, down the shore. We found the way without any trouble, reached there before sundown, played three games of cribbage, borrowed a dug-out and pulled back six miles to the upper camp. As we had eaten nothing since sunrise, we did not waste time in cooking our supper or in eating it, either. After supper we got out our pipes - built a rousing camp fire in the open air-established a faro bank (an institution of this country,) on our huge flat granite dining table, and bet white beans till one o'clock, when John went to bed. We were up before the sun the next morning, went out on the Lake and caught a fine trout for breakfast. But unfortunately, I spoilt part of the breakfast. We had coffee and tea boiling on the fire, in coffee-pots and fearing they might not be strong enough, I added more ground coffee, and more tea, but - you know mistakes will happen. - I put the tea in the coffee-pot, and the coffee in the teapot - and if you imagine that they were not villainous mixtures, just try the effect once.

And so Bella is to be married on the 1st of Oct. Well, I send her and her husband my very best wishes, and - I may not be here - but wherever I am on that night, we'll have a rousing camp-fire and a jollification in honor of the event.

In a day or two we shall probably go to the Lake and build another cabin and fence, and get everything into satisfactory trim before our trip to Esmeralda about the first of November.

What has become of Sam Bowen? I would give my last shirt to have him out here. I will make no promises, but I believe if John would give him a thousand dollars and send him out here he would not regret it. He might possibly do very well here, but he could do little without capital.

Remember me to all my St. Louis and Keokuk friends, and tell Challie and Hallie Renson that I heard a military band play "What are the Wild Waves Saying?" the other night, and it reminded me very forcibly of them. It brought Ella Creel and Belle across the Desert too in an instant, for they sang the song in Orion's yard the first time I ever heard it. It was like meeting an old friend. I tell you I could have swallowed that whole band, trombone and all, if such a compliment would have been any gratification to them.

Love to the young folks,

SAM.

The reference in the foregoing letter to Esmeralda has to do with mining plans. He was beginning to be mildly interested, and, with his brother Orion, had acquired "feet" in an Esmeralda camp, probably at a very small price - so small as to hold out no exciting prospect of riches. In his next letter he gives us the size of this claim, which he has visited. His interest, however, still appears to be chiefly in his timber claim on Lake Bigler (Tahoe), though we are never to hear of it again after this letter.

To Mrs. Moffett, in St. Louis:

CARSON CITY, Oct. 25, 1861.

MY DEAR SISTER, - I have just finished reading your letter and Ma's of Sept. 8th. How in the world could they have been so long coming? You ask me if I have for gotten my promise to lay a claim for Mr. Moffett. By no means. I have already laid a timber claim on the borders of a lake (Bigler) which throws Como in the shade - and if we succeed in getting one Mr. Jones, to move his saw-mill up there, Mr. Moffett can just consider that claim better than bank stock. Jones says he will move his mill up next spring. In that claim I took up about two miles in length by one in width - and the names in it are as follows: "Sam. L Clemens, Wm. A. Moffett, Thos. Nye" and three others. It is situated on "Sam Clemens Bay" - so named by Capt. Nye - and it goes by that name among the inhabitants of that region. I had better stop about "the Lake," though, - for whenever I think of it I want to go there and die, the place is so beautiful. I'll build a country seat there one of these days that will make the Devil's mouth water if he ever visits the earth. Jim Lampton will never know whether I laid a claim there for him or not until he comes here himself. We have now got about 1,650 feet of mining ground - and if it proves good, Mr. Moffett's name will go in - if not, I can get "feet" for him in the Spring which will be good. You see, Pamela, the trouble does not consist in getting mining ground - for that is plenty enough - but the money to work it with after you get it is the mischief. When I was in Esmeralda, a young fellow gave me fifty feet in the "Black Warrior" - an unprospected claim. The other day he wrote me that he had gone down eight feet on the ledge, and found it eight feet thick - and pretty good rock, too. He said he could take out rock now if there were a mill to crush it - but the mills are all engaged (there are only four of them) so, if I were willing, he would suspend work until Spring. I wrote him to let it alone at present - because, you see, in the Spring I can go down myself and help him look after it. There will then be twenty mills there. Orion and I have confidence enough in this country to think that if the war will let us alone we can make Mr. Moffett rich without its ever costing him a cent of money or particle of trouble. We shall lay plenty of claims for him, but if they never pay him anything, they will never cost him anything, Orion and I are not financiers. Therefore, you must persuade Uncle Jim to come out here and help us in that line. I have written to him twice to come. I wrote him today. In both letters I told him not to let you or Ma know that we dealt in such romantic nonsense as "brilliant prospects," because I always did hate for anyone to know what my plans or hopes or prospects were - for, if I kept people in ignorance in these matters, no one could be disappointed but myself, if they were not realized. You know I never told you that I went on the river under a promise to pay Bixby $500, until I had paid the money and cleared my skirts of the possibility of having my judgment criticised. I would not say anything about our prospects now, if we were nearer home. But I suppose at this distance you are more anxious than you would be if you saw us every month- and therefore it is hardly fair to keep you in the dark. However, keep these matters to yourselves, and then if we fail, we'll keep the laugh in the family.

What we want now is something that will commence paying immediately. We have got a chance to get into a claim where they say a tunnel has been run 150 feet, and the ledge struck. I got a horse yesterday, and went out with the Attorney-General and the claim-owner - and we tried to go to the claim by a new route, and got lost in the mountains - sunset overtook us before we found the claim - my horse got too lame to carry me, and I got down and drove him ahead of me till within four miles of town - then we sent Rice on ahead. Bunker, (whose horse was in good condition,) undertook, to lead mine, and I followed after him. Darkness shut him out from my view in less than a minute, and within the next minute I lost the road and got to wandering in the sage brush. I would find the road occasionally and then lose it again in a minute or so. I got to Carson about nine o'clock, at night, but not by the road I traveled when I left it. The General says my horse did very well for awhile, but soon refused to lead. Then he dismounted, and had a jolly time driving both horses ahead of him and chasing them here and there through the sage brush (it does my soul good when I think of it) until he got to town, when both animals deserted him, and he cursed them handsomely and came home alone. Of course the horses went to their stables.

Tell Sammy I will lay a claim for him, and he must come out and attend to it. He must get rid of that propensity for tumbling down, though, for when we get fairly started here, I don't think we shall have time to pick up those who fall.....

That is Stoughter's house, I expect, that Cousin Jim has moved into. This is just the country for Cousin Jim to live in. I don't believe it would take him six months to make $100,000 here, if he had 3,000 dollars to commence with. I suppose he can't leave his family though.

Tell Mrs. Benson I never intend to be a lawyer. I have been a slave several times in my life, but I'll never be one again. I always intend to be so situated (unless I marry,) that I can "pull up stakes" and clear out whenever I feel like it.

We are very thankful to you, Pamela, for the papers you send. We have received half a dozen or more, and, next to letters, they are the most welcome visitors we have.

Write oftener, Pamela.

Yr. Brother

SAM.

The "Cousin Jim" mentioned in this letter is the original of the character of Colonel Sellers. Whatever Mark Twain's later opinion of Cousin Jim Lampton's financial genius may have been, he seems to have respected it at this time.

More than three months pass until we have another letter, and in that time the mining fever had become well seated. Mark Twain himself was full of the Sellers optimism, and it was bound to overflow, fortify as he would against it.

He met with little enough encouragement. With three companions, in midwinter, he made a mining excursion to the much exploited Humboldt region, returning empty-handed after a month or two of hard experience. This is the trip picturesquely described in Chapters XXVII to XXXIII of Roughing It. - [It is set down historically in Mark Twain 'A Biography.' Harper & brothers.] - He, mentions the Humboldt in his next letter, but does not confess his failure.

To Mrs. Jane Clemens and Mrs. Moffett, in St. Louis:

CARSON CITY, Feb. 8, 1862.

MY DEAR MOTHER AND SISTER, - By George Pamela, I begin to fear that I have invoked a Spirit of some kind or other which I will find some difficulty in laying. I wasn't much terrified by your growing inclinations, but when you begin to call presentiments to your aid, I confess that I "weaken." Mr. Moffett is right, as I said before - and I am not much afraid of his going wrong. Men are easily dealt with - but when you get the women started, you are in for it, you know. But

I have decided on two things, viz: Any of you, or all of you, may live in California, for that is the Garden of Eden reproduced - but you shall never live in Nevada; and secondly, none of you, save Mr. Moffett, shall ever cross the Plains. If you were only going to Pike's Peak, a little matter of 700 miles from St. Jo, you might take the coach, and I wouldn't say a word. But I consider it over 2,000 miles from St. Jo to Carson, and the first 6 or 800 miles is mere Fourth of July, compared to the balance of the route. But Lord bless you, a man enjoys every foot of it. If you ever come here or to California, it must be by sea. Mr. Moffett must come by overland coach, though, by all means. He would consider it the jolliest little trip he ever took in his life. Either June, July, or August are the proper months to make the journey in. He could not suffer from heat, and three or four heavy army blankets would make the cold nights comfortable. If the coach were full of passengers, two good blankets would probably be sufficient. If he comes, and brings plenty of money, and fails to invest it to his entire satisfaction; I will prophesy no more.

But I will tell you a few things which you wouldn't have found out if I hadn't got myself into this scrape. I expect to return to St. Louis in July - per steamer. I don't say that I will return then, or that I shall be able to do it - but I expect to - you bet. I came down here from Humboldt, in order to look after our Esmeralda interests, and my sore-backed horse and the bad roads have prevented me from making the journey. Yesterday one of my old Esmeralda friends, Bob Howland, arrived here, and I have had a talk with him. He owns with me in the "Horatio and Derby" ledge. He says our tunnel is in 52 feet, and a small stream of water has been struck, which bids fair to become a "big thing" by the time the ledge is reached - sufficient to supply a mill. Now, if you knew anything of the value of water, here; you would perceive, at a glance that if the water should amount to 50 or 100 inches, we wouldn't care whether school kept or not. If the ledge should prove to be worthless, we'd sell the water for money enough to give us quite a lift. But you see, the ledge will not prove to be worthless. We have located, near by, a fine site for a mill; and when we strike the ledge, you know, we'll have a mill-site, water power, and pay-rock, all handy. Then we shan't care whether we have capital or not. Mill-folks will build us a mill, and wait for their pay. If nothing goes wrong, we'll strike the ledge in June - and if we do, I'll be home in July, you know.

Pamela, don't you know that undemonstrated human calculations won't do to bet on? Don't you know that I have only talked, as yet, but proved nothing? Don't you know that I have expended money in this country but have made none myself? Don't you know that I have never held in my hands a gold or silver bar that belonged to me? Don't you know that it's all talk and no cider so far? Don't you know that people who always feel jolly, no matter where they are or what happens to them - who have the organ of hope preposterously developed - who are endowed with an uncongealable sanguine temperament - who never feel concerned about the price of corn - and who cannot, by any possibility, discover any but the bright side of a picture - are very apt to go to extremes, and exaggerate with 40-horse microscopic power? Of course I never tried to raise these suspicions in your mind, but then your knowledge of the fact that some people's poor frail human nature is a sort of crazy institution anyhow, ought to have suggested them to you. Now, if I hadn't thoughtlessly got you into the notion of coming out here, and thereby got myself into a scrape, I wouldn't have given you that highly-colored paragraph about the mill, etc., because, you know, if that pretty little picture should fail, and wash out, and go the Devil generally, it wouldn't cost me the loss of an hour's sleep, but you fellows would be so much distressed on my account as I could possibly be if "circumstances beyond my control" were to prevent my being present at my own funeral. But - but -

"In the bright lexicon of youth,
There's no such word as Fail - "

and I'll prove it!

And look here. I came near forgetting it. Don't you say a word to me about "trains" across the plains. Because I am down on that arrangement. That sort of thing is "played out," you know. The Overland Coach or the Mail Steamer is the thing.

You want to know something about the route between California and Nevada Territory? Suppose you take my word for it, that it is exceedingly jolly. Or take, for a winter view, J. Ross Brown's picture, in Harper's Monthly, of pack mules tumbling fifteen hundred feet down the side of a mountain. Why bless you, there's scenery on that route. You can stand on some of those noble peaks and see Jerusalem and the Holy Land. And you can start a boulder, and send it tearing up the earth and crashing over trees-down-down-down-to the very devil, Madam. And you would probably stand up there and look, and stare and wonder at the magnificence spread out before you till you starved to death, if let alone. But you should take someone along to keep you moving.

Since you want to know, I will inform you that an eight-stamp water mill, put up and ready for business would cost about $10,000 to $12,000. Then, the water to run it with would cost from $1,000 to $30,000 - and even more, according to the location. What I mean by that, is, that water powers in THIS vicinity, are immensely valuable. So, also, in Esmeralda. But Humboldt is a new country, and things don't cost so much there yet. I saw a good water power sold there for $750.00. But here is the way the thing is managed. A man with a good water power on Carson river will lean his axe up against a tree (provided you find him chopping cord-wood at $4 a day,) and taking his chalk pipe out of his mouth to afford him an opportunity to answer your questions, will look you coolly in the face and tell you his little property is worth forty or fifty thousand dollars! But you can easily fix him. You tell him that you'll build a quartz mill on his property, and make him a fourth or a third, or half owner in said mill in consideration of the privilege of using said property - and that will bring him to his milk in a jiffy. So he spits on his hands, and goes in again with his axe, until the mill is finished, when lo! out pops the quondam wood-chopper, arrayed in purple and fine linen, and prepared to deal in bank-stock, or bet on the races, or take government loans, with an air, as to the amount, of the most don't care-a-d - dest unconcern that you can conceive of. By George, if I just had a thousand dollars - I'd be all right! Now there's the "Horatio," for instance. There are five or six shareholders in it, and I know I could buy half of their interests at, say $20 per foot, now that flour is worth $50 per barrel and they are pressed for money. But I am hard up myself, and can't buy - and in June they'll strike the ledge and then "good-bye canary." I can't get it for love or money. Twenty dollars a foot! Think of it. For ground that is proven to be rich. Twenty dollars, Madam - and we wouldn't part with a foot of our 75 for five times the sum. So it will be in Humboldt next summer. The boys will get pushed and sell ground for a song that is worth a fortune. But I am at the helm, now. I have convinced Orion that he hasn't business talent enough to carry on a peanut stand, and he has solemnly promised me that he will meddle no more with mining, or other matters not connected with the Secretary's office. So, you see, if mines are to be bought or sold, or tunnels run, or shafts sunk, parties have to come to me - and me only. I'm the "firm," you know.

"How long does it take one of those infernal trains to go through?" Well, anywhere between three and five months.

Tell Margaret that if you ever come to live in California, that you can promise her a home for a hundred years, and a bully one - but she wouldn't like the country. Some people are malicious enough to think that if the devil were set at liberty and told to confine himself to Nevada Territory, that he would come here - and look sadly around, awhile, and then get homesick and go back to hell again. But I hardly believe it, you know. I am saying, mind you, that Margaret wouldn't like the country, perhaps - nor the devil either, for that matter, or any other man but I like it. When it rains here, it never lets up till it has done all the raining it has got to do - and after that, there's a dry spell, you bet. Why, I have had my whiskers and moustaches so full of alkali dust that you'd have thought I worked in a starch factory and boarded in a flour barrel.

Since we have been here there has not been a fire -

although the houses are built of wood. They "holler" fire sometimes, though, but I am always too late to see the smoke before the fire is out, if they ever have any. Now they raised a yell here in front of the office a moment ago. I put away my papers, and locked up everything of value, and changed my boots, and pulled off my coat, and went and got a bucket of water, and came back to see what the matter was, remarking to myself, "I guess I'll be on hand this time, any way." But I met a friend on the pavement, and he said, "Where you been? Fire's out half an hour ago."

Ma says Axtele was above "suspition" - but I have searched through Webster's Unabridged, and can't find the word. However, it's of no consequence - I hope he got down safely. I knew Axtele and his wife as well as I know Dan Haines. Mrs. A. once tried to embarrass me in the presence of company by asking me to name her baby, when she was well aware that I didn't know the sex of that Phenomenon. But I told her to call it Frances, and spell it to suit herself. That was about nine years ago, and Axtele had no property, and could hardly support his family by his earnings. He was a pious cuss, though. Member of Margaret Sexton's Church.

And Ma says "it looks like a man can't hold public office and be honest." Why, certainly not, Madam. A man can't hold public office and be honest. Lord bless you, it is a common practice with Orion to go about town stealing little things that happen to be lying around loose. And I don't remember having heard him speak the truth since we have been in Nevada. He even tries to prevail upon me to do these things, Ma, but I wasn't brought up in that way, you know. You showed the public what you could do in that line when you raised me, Madam. But then you ought to have raised me first, so that Orion could have had the benefit of my example. Do you know that he stole all the stamps out of an 8 stamp quartz mill one night, and brought them home under his over-coat and hid them in the back room?

Yrs. etc.,

SAM

A little later he had headed for the Esmeralda Hills. Some time in February he was established there in a camp with a young man by the name of Horatio Phillips (Raish). Later he camped with Bob Howland, who, as City Marshal of Aurora, became known as the most fearless man in the Territory, and, still later, with Calvin H. Higbie (Cal), to whom 'Roughing It' would one day be dedicated. His own funds were exhausted by this time, and Orion, with his rather slender salary, became the financial partner of the firm.

It was a comfortless life there in the Esmeralda camp. Snow covered everything. There was nothing to do, and apparently nothing to report; for there are no letters until April. Then the first one is dated Carson City, where he seems to be making a brief sojourn. It is a rather heavy attempt to be light-hearted; its playfulness suggests that of a dancing bear.

To Mrs. Jane Clemens, in St. Louis:

CARSON CITY, April 2, 1862.

MY DEAR MOTHER, - Yours of March 2nd has just been received. I see I am in for it again - with Annie. But she ought to know that I was always stupid. She used to try to teach me lessons from the Bible, but I never could understand them. Doesn't she remember telling me the story of Moses, one Sunday, last Spring, and how hard she tried to explain it and simplify it so that I could understand it - but I couldn't? And how she said it was strange that while her ma and her grandma and her uncle Orion could understand anything in the world, I was so dull that I couldn't understand the "easiest thing?" And doesn't she remember that finally a light broke in upon me and I said it was all right - that I knew old Moses himself - and that he kept a clothing store in Market Street? And then she went to her ma and said she didn't know what would become of her uncle Sam he was too dull to learn anything - ever! And I'm just as dull yet. Now I have no doubt her letter was spelled right, and was correct in all particulars - but then I had to read it according to my lights; and they being inferior, she ought to overlook the mistakes I make specially, as it is not my fault that I wasn't born with good sense. I am sure she will detect an encouraging ray of intelligence in that last argument.....

I am waiting here, trying to rent a better office for Orion. I have got the refusal after next week of a room on first floor of a fire-proof brick-rent, eighteen hundred dollars a year. Don't know yet whether we can get it or not. If it is not rented before the week is up, we can.

I was sorry to hear that Dick was killed. I gave him his first lesson in the musket drill. We had half a dozen muskets in our office when it was over Isbell's Music Rooms.
I hope I am wearing the last white shirt that will embellish my person for many a day - for I do hope that I shall be out of Carson long before this reaches you.

Love to all.

Very Respectfully

SAM.

The "Annie" in this letter was his sister Pamela's little daughter; long years after, she would be the wife of Charles L. Webster, Mark Twain's publishing partner. "Dick" the reader may remember as Dick Hingham, of the Keokuk printing-office; he was killed in charging the works at Fort Donelson.

Clemens was back in Esmeralda when the next letter was written, and we begin now to get pictures of that cheerless mining-camp, and to know something of the alternate hopes and discouragements of the hunt for gold - the miner one day soaring on wings of hope, on the next becoming excited, irritable, profane. The names of new mines appear constantly and vanish almost at a touch, suggesting the fairy-like evanescence of their riches.

But a few of the letters here will best speak for themselves; not all of them are needed. It is perhaps unnecessary to say that there is no intentional humor in these documents.

To Orion Clemens, in Carson City:

ESMERALDA, 13th April, 1862.

MY DEAR BROTHER, - Wasson got here night before last "from the wars." Tell Lockhart he is not wounded and not killed - is altogether unhurt. He says the whites left their stone fort before he and Lieut. Noble got there. A large amount of provisions and ammunition, which they left behind them, fell into the hands of the Indians. They had a pitched battle with the savages some fifty miles from the fort, in which Scott (sheriff) and another man was killed. This was the day before the soldiers came up with them. I mean Noble's men, and those under Cols. Evans and Mayfield, from Los Angeles. Evans assumed the chief command - and next morning the forces were divided into three parties, and marched against the enemy. Col. Mayfield was killed, and Sergeant Gillespie, also Noble's colonel was wounded. The California troops went back home, and Noble remained, to help drive the stock over here. And, as Cousin Sally Dillard says, this is all I know about the fight.

Work not yet begun on the H. and Derby - haven't seen it yet. It is still in the snow. Shall begin on it within 3 or 4 weeks - strike the ledge in July. Guess it is good - worth from $30 to $50 a foot in California.

Why didn't you send the "Live Yankee" deed-the very one I wanted? Have made no inquiries about it, much. Don't intend to until I get the deed. Send it along - by mail - d - n the Express - have to pay three times for all express matter; once in Carson and twice here. I don't expect to take the saddle-bags out of the express office. I paid twenty-five cts. for the Express deeds.

Man named Gebhart shot here yesterday while trying to defend a claim on Last Chance Hill. Expect he will die.

These mills here are not worth a d - n-except Clayton's - and it is not in full working trim yet.

Send me $40 or $50 - by mail - immediately.

The Red Bird is probably good - can't work on the tunnel on account of snow. The "Pugh" I have thrown away - shan't re-locate it. It is nothing but bed-rock croppings - too much work to find the ledge, if there is one. Shan't record the "Farnum" until I know more about it - perhaps not at all.

"Governor" under the snow.

"Douglas" and "Red Bird" are both recorded.

I have had opportunities to get into several ledges, but refused all but three - expect to back out of two of them.

Stir yourself as much as possible, and lay up $100 or $15,000, subject to my call. I go to work to-morrow, with pick and shovel. Something's got to come, by G - , before I let go, here.

Col. Youngs says you must rent Kinkead's room by all means - Government would rather pay $150 a month for your office than $75 for Gen. North's. Says you are playing your hand very badly, for either the Government's good opinion or anybody's else, in keeping your office in a shanty. Says put Gov. Nye in your place and he would have a stylish office, and no objections would ever be made, either. When old Col. Youngs talks this way, I think it time to get a fine office. I wish you would take that office, and fit it up handsomely, so that I can omit telling people that by this time you are handsomely located, when I know it is no such thing.

I am living with "Ratio Phillips." Send him one of those black portfolios - by the stage, and put a couple of pen-holders and a dozen steel pens in it.

If you should have occasion to dispose of the long desk before I return, don't forget to break open the middle drawer and take out my things. Envelop my black cloth coat in a newspaper and hang it in the back room.

Don't buy anything while I am here - but save up some money for me. Don't send any money home. I shall have your next quarter's salary spent before you get it, I think. I mean to make or break here within the next two or three months.

Yrs.

SAM

The "wars" mentioned in the opening paragraph of this letter were incident to the trouble concerning the boundary line between California and Nevada. The trouble continued for some time, with occasional bloodshed. The next letter is an exultant one. There were few enough of this sort. We cannot pretend to keep track of the multiplicity of mines and shares which lure the gold-hunters, pecking away at the flinty ledges, usually in the snow. It has been necessary to abbreviate this letter, for much of it has lost all importance with the years, and is merely confusing. Hope is still high in the writer's heart, and confidence in his associates still unshaken. Later he was to lose faith in "Raish," whether with justice or not we cannot know now.

To Orion Clowns, in Carson City:

ESMERALDA, May 11, 1862.

MY DEAR BRO, - TO use a French expression I have "got my d - d satisfy" at last. Two years' time will make us capitalists, in spite of anything. Therefore, we need fret and fume, and worry and doubt no more, but just lie still and put up with privations for six months. Perhaps three months will "let us out." Then, if Government refuses to pay the rent on your new office we can do it ourselves. We have got to wait six weeks, anyhow, for a dividend, maybe longer - but that it will come there is no shadow of a doubt, I have got the thing sifted down to a dead moral certainty. I own one-eighth of the new "Monitor Ledge, Clemens Company," and money can't buy a foot of it; because I know it to contain our fortune. The ledge is six feet wide, and one needs no glass to see gold and silver in

Mark Twain

it. Phillips and I own one half of a segregated claim in the "Flyaway" discovery, and good interests in two extensions on it. We put men to work on our part of the discovery yesterday, and last night they brought us some fine specimens. Rock taken from ten feet below the surface on the other part of the discovery, has yielded $150.00 to the ton in the mill and we are at work 300 feet from their shaft.

May 12 - Yours by the mail received last night. "Eighteen hundred feet in the C. T. Rice's Company!" Well, I am glad you did not accept of the 200 feet. Tell Rice to give it to some poor man.

But hereafter, when anybody holds up a glittering prospect before you, just argue in this wise, viz: That, if all spare change be devoted to working the "Monitor" and "Flyaway," 12 months, or 24 at furthest, will find all our earthly wishes satisfied, so far as money is concerned - and the more "feet" we have, the more anxiety we must bear - therefore, why not say "No - d - n your 'prospects,' I wait on a sure thing - and a man is less than a man, if he can't wait 2 years for a fortune?" When you and I came out here, we did not expect '63 or '64 to find us rich men - and if that proposition had been made, we would have accepted it gladly. Now, it is made.

Well, I am willing, now, that "Neary's tunnel," or anybody else's tunnel shall succeed. Some of them may beat us a few months, but we shall be on hand in the fullness of time, as sure as fate. I would hate to swap chances with any member of the "tribe" - in fact, I am so lost to all sense and reason as to be capable of refusing to trade "Flyaway" (with but 200 feet in the Company of four,) foot for foot for that splendid "Lady

Washington," with its lists of capitalist proprietors, and its 35,000 feet of Priceless ground.

I wouldn't mind being in some of those Clear Creek claims, if I lived in Carson and we could spare the money. But I have struck my tent in Esmeralda, and I care for no mines but those which I can superintend myself. I am a citizen here now, and I am satisfied - although R. and I are strapped and we haven't three days' rations in the house.

Raish is looking anxiously for money and so am I. Send me whatever you can spare conveniently - I want it to work the Flyaway with. My fourth of that claim only cost me $50, (which isn't paid yet, though,) and I suppose I could sell it here in town for ten times that amount today, but I shall probably hold onto it till the cows come home. I shall work the "Monitor" and the other claims with my own hands. I prospected of a pound of "M," yesterday, and Raish reduced it with the blow-pipe, and got about ten or twelve cents in gold and silver, besides the other half of it which we spilt on the floor and didn't get. The specimen came from the croppings, but was a choice one, and showed much free gold to the naked eye.

Well, I like the corner up-stairs office amazingly - provided, it has one fine, large front room superbly carpeted, for the safe and a $150 desk, or such a matter - one handsome room amidships, less handsomely gotten up, perhaps, for records and consultations, and one good-sized bedroom and adjoining it a kitchen, neither of which latter can be entered by anybody but yourself - and finally, when one of the ledges begins to pay, the whole to be kept in parlor order by two likely contrabands at big wages, the same to be free of expense to the Government. You want the entire second story - no less room than you would have had in Harris and Co's. Make them fix for you before the 1st of July-for maybe you might want to "come out strong" on the 4th, you know.

No, the Post Office is all right and kept by a gentleman but W. F. Express isn't. They charge 25 cts to express a letter from here, but I believe they have quit charging twice for letters that arrive prepaid.

The "Flyaway" specimen I sent you, (taken by myself from DeKay's shaft, 300 feet from where we are going to sink) cannot be called "choice," exactly - say something above medium, to be on the safe side. But I have seen exceedingly choice chunks from that shaft. My intention at first in sending the Antelope specimen was that you might see that it resembles the Monitor - but, come to think, a man can tell absolutely nothing about that without seeing both ledges themselves. I tried to break a handsome chunk from a huge piece of my darling Monitor which we brought from the croppings yesterday, but it all splintered up, and I send you the scraps. I call that "choice" - any d - d fool would. Don't ask if it has been assayed, for it hasn't. It don't need it. It is amply able to speak for itself. It is six feet wide on top, and traversed through and through with veins whose color proclaims their worth. What the devil does a man want with any more feet when he owns in the Flyaway and the invincible bomb-proof Monitor?

If I had anything more to say I have forgotten what it was, unless, perhaps, that I want a sum of money - anywhere from $20 to $150, as soon as possible.

Raish sends regards. He or I, one will drop a line to the "Age" occasionally. I suppose you saw my letters in the "Enterprise."

Yr. BRO,

SAM

P. S. I suppose Pamela never will regain her health, but she could improve it by coming to California - provided the trip didn't kill her.

You see Bixby is on the flag-ship. He always was the best pilot on the Mississippi, and deserves his "posish." They have done a reckless thing, though, in putting Sam Bowen on the "Swan" - for if a bomb-shell happens to come his way, he will infallibly jump overboard.

Send me another package of those envelopes, per Bagley's coat pocket.

We see how anxious he was for his brother to make a good official showing. If a niggardly Government refused to provide decent quarters - no matter; the miners, with gold pouring in, would themselves pay for a suite "superbly carpeted," and all kept in order by "two likely contrabands" - that is to say, negroes. Samuel Clemens in those days believed in expansion and impressive surroundings. His brother, though also mining mad, was rather inclined to be penny wise in the matter of office luxury - not a bad idea, as it turned out.

Orion, by the way, was acquiring "feet" on his own account, and in one instance, at least, seems to have won his brother's commendation.

The 'Enterprise' letters mentioned we shall presently hear of again.

To Orion Clemens, in Carson City:

ESMERALDA, Sunday, May - , 1862.

MY DEAR BROTHER, - Well, if you haven't "struck it rich - "that is, if the piece of rock you sent me came from a bona fide ledge - and it looks as if it did. If that is a ledge, and you own 200 feet in it, why, it's a big thing - and I have nothing more to say. If you have actually made something by helping to pay somebody's prospecting expenses it is a wonder of the first magnitude, and deserves to rank as such.

If that rock came from a well-defined ledge, that particular vein must be at least an inch wide, judging from this specimen, which is fully that thick.

When I came in the other evening, hungry and tired and ill-natured, and threw down my pick and shovel, Raish gave me your specimen - said Bagley brought it, and asked me if it were cinnabar. I examined it by the waning daylight, and took the specks of fine gold for sulphurets - wrote you I did not think much of it - and posted the letter immediately.

But as soon as I looked at it in the broad light of day, I saw my mistake. During the week, we have made three horns, got a blow-pipe, &c, and yesterday, all prepared, we prospected the "Mountain House." I broke the specimen in two, and found it full of fine gold inside. Then we washed out one-fourth of it, and got a noble prospect. This we reduced with the blow-pipe, and got about two cents (herewith enclosed) in pure gold.

As the fragment prospected weighed rather less than an ounce, this would give about $500 to the ton. We were eminently well satisfied. Therefore, hold on to the "Mountain House," for it is a "big thing." Touch it lightly, as far as money is concerned, though, for it is well to reserve the code of justice in the matter of quartz ledges - that is, consider them all (and their owners) guilty (of "shenanigan") until they are proved innocent.

P. S. - Monday - Ratio and I have bought one-half of a segregated claim in the original "Flyaway," for $100 - $50 down. We haven't a cent in the house. We two will work the ledge, and have full control, and pay all expenses. If you can spare $100 conveniently, let me have it - or $50, anyhow, considering that I own one fourth of this, it is of course more valuable than one 1/7 of the "Mountain House," although not so rich ....

There is too much of a sameness in the letters of this period to use all of them. There are always new claims, and work done, apparently without system or continuance, hoping to uncover sudden boundless affluence.

In the next letter and the one following it we get a hint of an episode, or rather of two incidents which he combined into an episode in Roughing It. The story as told in that book is an account of what might have happened, rather than history. There was never really any money in the "blind lead" of the Wide West claim, except that which was sunk in it by unfortunate investors. Only extracts from these letters are given. The other portions are irrelevant and of slight value.

Extract from a letter to Orion Clemens, in Carson City: 1862.

Two or three of the old "Salina" company entered our hole on the Monitor yesterday morning, before our men got there, and took possession, armed with revolvers. And according to the d - d laws of this forever d - d country, nothing but the District Court (and there ain't any) can touch the matter, unless it assumes the shape of an infernal humbug which they call "forcible entry and detainer," and in order to bring that about, you must compel the jumpers to use personal violence toward you! We went up and demanded possession, and they refused. Said they were in the hole, armed and meant to die for it, if necessary.

I got in with them, and again demanded possession. They said I might stay in it as long as I pleased, and work but they would do the same. I asked one of our company to take my place in the hole, while I went to consult a lawyer. He did so. The lawyer said it was no go. They must offer some "force."

Our boys will try to be there first in the morning - in which case they may get possession and keep it. Now you understand the shooting scrape in which Gebhart was killed the other day. The Clemens Company - all of us - hate to resort to arms in this matter, and it will not be done until it becomes a forced hand - but I think that will be the end of it, never-the-less.

The mine relocated in this letter was not the "Wide West," but it furnished the proper incident. The only mention of the "Wide West" is found in a letter written in July.

Extract from a letter to Orion Clemens, in Carson City: 1862

If I do not forget it, I will send you, per next mail, a pinch of decom. (decomposed rock) which I pinched with thumb and finger from "Wide West" ledge awhile ago. Raish and I have secured 200 out of a 400 ft. in it, which perhaps (the ledge, I mean) is a spur from the W. W. - our shaft is about 100 ft. from the W. W. shaft. In order to get in, we agreed to sink 30 ft. We have sub-let to another man for 50 ft., and we pay for powder and sharpening tools.

The "Wide West" claim was forfeited, but there is no evidence to show that Clemens and his partners were ever, except in fiction, "millionaires for ten days." The background, the local color, and the possibilities are all real enough, but Mark Twain's aim in this, as in most of his other reminiscent writing, was to arrange and adapt his facts to the needs of a good story.

The letters of this summer (1862) most of them bear evidence of waning confidence in mining as a source of fortune - the miner has now little faith in his own judgment, and none at all in that of his brother, who was without practical experience.

Letter to Orion Clemens, in Carson City:

ESMERALDA, Thursday.

MY DEAR BRO., - Yours of the 17th, per express, just received. Part of it pleased me exceedingly, and part of it didn't. Concerning the letter, for instance: You have PROMISED me that you would leave all mining matters, and everything involving an outlay of money, in my hands.

Sending a man fooling around the country after ledges, for God's sake! when there are hundreds of feet of them under my nose here, begging for owners, free of charge. I don't want any more feet, and I won't touch another foot - so you see, Orion, as far as any ledges of Perry's are concerned, (or any other except what I examine first with my own eyes,) I freely yield my right to share ownership with you.

The balance of your letter, I say, pleases me exceedingly. Especially that about the H. and D. being worth from $30 to $50 in Cal. It pleases me because, if the ledges prove to be worthless, it will be a pleasant reflection to know that others were beaten worse than ourselves. Raish sold a man 30 feet, yesterday, at $20 a foot, although I was present at the sale, and told the man the ground wasn't worth a d - n. He said he had been hankering after a few feet in the H. and D. for a long time, and he had got them at last, and he couldn't help thinking he had secured a good thing. We went and looked at the ledges, and both of them acknowledged that there was nothing in them but good "indications." Yet the owners in the H. and D. will part with anything else sooner than with feet in these ledges. Well, the work goes slowly - very slowly on, in the tunnel, and we'll strike it some day. But - if we "strike it rich," - I've lost my guess, that's all. I expect that the way it got so high in Cal. was, that Raish's brother, over there was offered $750.00 for 20 feet of it, and he refused .....

Couldn't go on the hill today. It snowed. It always snows here, I expect.

Don't you suppose they have pretty much quit writing, at home?

When you receive your next 1/4 yr's salary, don't send any of it here until after you have told me you have got it. Remember this. I am afraid of that H. and D.

They have struck the ledge in the Live Yankee tunnel, and I told the President, Mr. Allen, that it wasn't as good as the croppings. He said that was true enough, but they would hang to it until it did prove rich. He is much of a gentleman, that man Allen.

And ask Gaslerie why the devil he don't send along my commission as Deputy Sheriff. The fact of my being in California, and out of his country, wouldn't amount to a d - n with me, in the performance of my official duties.

I have nothing to report, at present, except that I shall find out all I want to know about this locality before I leave it.

How do the Records pay?

Yr. Bro.

SAM.

In one of the foregoing letters - the one dated May 11 there is a reference to the writer's "Enterprise Letters." Sometimes, during idle days in the camp, the miner had followed old literary impulses and written an occasional burlesque sketch, which he had signed "Josh," and sent to the Territorial Enterprise, at Virginia City. - [One contribution was sent to a Keokuk paper, The Gate City, and a letter written by Mrs. Jane Clemens at the time would indicate that Mark Twain's mother did not always approve of her son's literary efforts. She hopes that he will do better, and some time write something "that his kin will be proud of."] - The rough, vigorous humor of these had attracted some attention, and Orion, pleased with any measure of success that might come to his brother, had allowed the authorship of them to become known. When, in July, the financial situation became desperate, the Esmeralda miner was moved to turn to literature for relief. But we will let him present the situation himself.

To Orion Clemens, in Carson City:

ESMERALDA, July 23d, 1862.

MY DEAR BRO., - No, I don't own a foot in the "Johnson" ledge - I will tell the story some day in a more intelligible manner than Tom has told it. You needn't take the trouble to deny Tom's version, though. I own 25 feet (1-16) of the 1st east ex. on it - and Johnson himself has contracted to find the ledge for 100 feet. Contract signed yesterday. But as the ledge will be difficult to find he is allowed six months to find it in. An eighteenth of the Ophir was a fortune to John D. Winters - and the Ophir can't beat the Johnson any.....

My debts are greater than I thought for; I bought $25 worth of clothing, and sent $25 to Higbie, in the cement diggings. I owe about $45 or $50, and have got about $45 in my pocket. But how in the h - l I am going to live on something over $100 until October or November, is singular. The fact is, I must have something to do, and that shortly, too.....

Now write to the Sacramento Union folks, or to Marsh, and tell them I'll write as many letters a week as they want, for $10 a week - my board must be paid. Tell them I have corresponded with the N. Orleans Crescent, and other papers - and the Enterprise. California is full of people who have interests here, and it's d - d seldom they hear from this country. I can't write a specimen letter - now, at any rate - I'd rather undertake to write a Greek poem. Tell 'em the mail and express leave three times a week, and it costs from 25 to 50 cents to send letters by the blasted express. If they want letters from here, who'll run from morning till night collecting materials cheaper. I'll write a short letter twice a week, for the present, for the "Age," for $5 per week. Now it has been a long time since I couldn't make my own living, and it shall be a long time before I loaf another year.....

If I get the other 25 feet in the Johnson ex., I shan't care a d - n. I'll be willing to curse awhile and wait. And if I can't move the bowels of those hills this fall, I will come up and clerk for you until I get money enough to go over the mountains for the winter.

Yr. Bro.

SAM.

The Territorial Enterprise at Virginia City was at this time owned by Joseph T. Goodman, who had bought it on the eve of the great Comstock silver-mining boom, and from a struggling, starving sheet had converted it into one of the most important - certainly the most picturesque-papers on the coast. The sketches which the Esmeralda miner had written over the name of "Josh" fitted into it exactly, and when a young man named Barstow, in the business office, urged Goodman to invite "Josh" to join their staff, the Enterprise owner readily fell in with the idea. Among a lot of mining matters of no special interest, Clemens, July 3oth, wrote his brother: "Barstow has offered me *the post as local reporter for the Enterprise at $25 a week, and I have written him that I will let him know next mail, if possible."*

In Roughing It we are told that the miner eagerly accepted the proposition to come to Virginia City, but the letters tell a different story. Mark Twain was never one to abandon any undertaking easily. His unwillingness to surrender in a lost cause would cost him more than one fortune in the years to come. A week following the date of the foregoing he was still undecided.

To Orion Clemens, in Carson City:

ESMERALDA, Aug. 7, 1862.

MY DEAR BRO, - Barstow wrote that if I wanted the place I could have it. I wrote him that I guessed I would take it, and asked him how long before I must come up there. I have not heard from him since.

Now, I shall leave at mid-night tonight, alone and on foot for a walk of 60 or 70 miles through a totally uninhabited country, and it is barely possible that mail facilities may prove infernally "slow" during the few weeks I expect to spend out there. But do you write Barstow that I have left here for a week or so, and in case he should want me he must write me here, or let me know through you.

The Contractors say they will strike the Fresno next week. After fooling with those assayers a week, they concluded not to buy "Mr. Flower" at $50, although they would have given five times the sum for it four months ago. So I have made out a deed for one half of all Johnny's ground and acknowledged and left in judge F. K. Becktel's hands, and if judge Turner wants it he must write to Becktel and pay him his Notary fee of $1.50. I would have paid that fee myself, but I want money now as I leave town tonight. However, if you think it isn't right, you can pay the fee to judge Turner yourself.

Hang to your money now. I may want some when I get back.....

See that you keep out of debt-to anybody. Bully for B.! Write him that I would write him myself, but I am to take a walk tonight and haven't time. Tell him to bring his family out with him. He can rely upon what I say - and I say the land has lost its ancient desolate appearance; the rose and the oleander have taken the place of the departed sage-bush; a rich black loam, garnished with moss, and flowers, and the greenest of grass, smiles to Heaven from the vanished sand-plains; the "endless snows" have all disappeared, and in their stead, or to repay us for their loss, the mountains rear their billowy heads aloft, crowned with a fadeless and eternal verdure; birds, and fountains, and trees-tropical bees - everywhere! - and the poet dreamt of Nevada when he wrote:

> "and Sharon waves, in solemn praise,
> Her silent groves of palm."

and today the royal Raven listens in a dreamy stupor to the songs of the thrush and the nightingale and the canary - and shudders when the gaudy - plumaged birds of the distant South sweep by him to the orange groves of Carson. Tell him he wouldn't recognize the d - d country. He should bring his family by all means.

I intended to write home, but I haven't done it.

Yr. Bro.

 SAM.

In this letter we realize that he had gone into the wilderness to reflect - to get a perspective on the situation. He was a great walker in those days, and sometimes with Higbie, sometimes alone, made long excursions. One such is recorded in Roughing It, the trip to Mono Lake. We have no means of knowing where his seventy-mile tour led him now, but it is clear that he still had not reached a decision on his return. Indeed, we gather that he is inclined to keep up the battle among the barren Esmeralda hills.

Last mining letter; written to Mrs. Moffett, in St. Louis:

ESMERALDA, CAL., Aug. 15, 1862.

MY DEAR SISTER,-I mailed a letter to you and Ma this morning, but since then I have received yours to Orion and me. Therefore, I must answer right away, else I may leave town without doing it at all. What in thunder are pilot's wages to me? which question, I beg humbly to observe, is of a general nature, and not discharged particularly at you. But it is singular, isn't it, that such a matter should interest Orion, when it is of no earthly consequence to me? I never have once thought of returning home to go on the river again, and I never expect to do any more piloting at any price. My livelihood must be made in this country - and if I have to wait longer than I expected, let it be so - I have no fear of failure. You know I have extravagant hopes, for Orion tells you everything which he ought to keep to himself - but it's his nature to do that sort of thing, and I let him alone. I did think for awhile of going home this fall - but when I found that that was and had been the cherished intention and the darling aspiration every year, of these old care-worn Californians for twelve weary years - I felt a little uncomfortable, but I stole a march on Disappointment and said I would not go home this fall. I will spend the winter in San Francisco, if possible. Do not tell any one that I had any idea of piloting again at present - for it is all a mistake. This country suits me, and - it shall suit me, whether or no....

Dan Twing and I and Dan's dog, "cabin" together - and will continue to do so for awhile - until I leave for -

The mansion is 10x12, with a "domestic" roof. Yesterday it rained - the first shower for five months. "Domestic," it appears to me, is not water-proof. We went outside to keep from getting wet. Dan makes the bed when it is his turn to do it - and when it is my turn, I don't, you know. The dog is not a good hunter, and he isn't worth shucks to watch - but he scratches up the dirt floor of the cabin, and catches flies, and makes himself generally useful in the way of washing dishes. Dan gets up first in the morning and makes a fire - and I get up last and sit by it, while he cooks breakfast. We have a cold lunch at noon, and I cook supper - very much against my will. However, one must have one good meal a day, and if I were to live on Dan's abominable cookery, I should lose my appetite, you know. Dan attended Dr. Chorpenning's funeral yesterday, and he felt as though he ought to wear a white shirt - and we had a jolly good time finding such an article. We turned over all our traps, and he found one at last - but I shall always think it was suffering from yellow fever. He also found an old black coat, greasy, and wrinkled to that degree that it appeared to have been quilted at some time or other. In this gorgeous costume he attended the funeral. And when he returned, his own dog drove him away from the cabin, not recognizing him. This is true.

You would not like to live in a country where flour was $40 a barrel? Very well; then, I suppose you would not like to live here, where flour was $100 a barrel when I first came here. And shortly afterwards, it couldn't be had at any price - and for one month the people lived on barley, beans and beef - and nothing beside. Oh, no - we didn't luxuriate then! Perhaps not. But we said wise and severe things about the vanity and wickedness of high living. We preached our doctrine and practiced it. Which course I respectfully recommend to the clergymen of St. Louis.

Where is Beack Jolly? - [a pilot] - and Bixby?

Your Brother

SAM.

IV. LETTERS 1863-64. "MARK TWAIN."

COMSTOCK JOURNALISM. ARTEMUS WARD

There is a long hiatus in the correspondence here. For a space of many months there is but one letter to continue the story. Others were written, of course, but for some reason they have not survived. It was about the end of August (1862) when the miner finally abandoned the struggle, and with his pack on his shoulders walked the one and thirty miles over the mountains to Virginia City, arriving dusty, lame, and travel-stained to claim at last his rightful inheritance. At the Enterprise office he was welcomed, and in a brief time entered into his own. Goodman, the proprietor, himself a man of great ability, had surrounded himself with a group of gay-hearted fellows, whose fresh, wild way of writing delighted the Comstock pioneers far more than any sober presentation of mere news. Samuel Clemens fitted exactly into this group. By the end of the year he had become a leader of it. When he asked to be allowed to report the coming Carson legislature, Goodman consented, realizing that while Clemens knew nothing of parliamentary procedure, he would at least make the letters picturesque.

It was in the midst of this work that he adopted the name which he was to make famous throughout the world. The story of its adoption has been fully told elsewhere and need not be repeated here. - [See Mark Twain: A Biography, by the same author; Chapter XL.]

"Mark Twain" was first signed to a Carson letter, February 2, 1863, and from that time was attached to all of Samuel Clemens's work. The letters had already been widely copied, and the name now which gave them personality quickly obtained vogue. It was attached to himself as well as to the letters; heretofore he had been called Sam or Clemens, now he became almost universally Mark Twain and Mark.

This early period of Mark Twain's journalism is full of delicious history, but we are permitted here to retell only such of it as will supply connection to the infrequent letters. He wrote home briefly in February, but the letter contained nothing worth preserving. Then two months later he gives us at least a hint of his employment.

To Mrs. Jane Clemens and Mrs. Moffett, in St. Louis:

VIRGINIA, April 11, 1863.

MY DEAR MOTHER AND SISTER, - It is very late at night, and I am writing in my room, which is not quite as large or as nice as the one I had at home. My board, washing and lodging cost me seventy-five dollars a month.

I have just received your letter, Ma, from Carson - the one in which you doubt my veracity about the statements I made in a letter to you. That's right. I don't recollect what the statements were, but I suppose they were mining statistics. I have just finished writing up my report for the morning paper, and giving the Unreliable a column of advice about how to conduct himself in church, and now I will tell you a few more lies, while my hand is in. For instance, some of the boys made me a present of fifty feet in the East India G. and S. M. Company ten days ago. I was offered ninety-five dollars a foot for it, yesterday, in gold. I refused it - not because I think the claim is worth a cent for I don't but because I had a curiosity to see how high it would go, before people find out how worthless it is. Besides, what if one mining claim does fool me? I have got plenty more. I am not in a particular hurry to get rich. I suppose I couldn't well help getting rich here some time or other, whether I wanted to or not. You folks do not believe in Nevada, and I am glad you don't. Just keep on thinking so.

I was at the Gould and Curry mine, the other day, and they had two or three tons of choice rock piled up, which was valued at $20,000 a ton. I gathered up a hat-full of chunks, on account of their beauty as specimens - they don't let everybody supply themselves so liberally. I send Mr. Moffett a little specimen of it for his cabinet. If you don't know what the white stuff on it is, I must inform you that it is purer silver than the minted coin. There is about as much gold in it as there is silver, but it is not visible. I will explain to you some day how to detect it.

Pamela, you wouldn't do for a local reporter - because you don't appreciate the interest that attaches to names.

An item is of no use unless it speaks of some person, and not then, unless that person's name is distinctly mentioned. The most interesting letter one can write, to an absent friend, is one that treats of persons he has been acquainted with rather than the public events of the day. Now you speak of a young lady who wrote to Hollie Benson that she had seen me; and you didn't mention her name. It was just a mere chance that I ever guessed who she was - but I did, finally, though I don't remember her name, now. I was introduced to her in San Francisco by Hon. A. B. Paul, and saw her afterwards in Gold Hill. They were a very pleasant lot of girls - she and her sisters.

P. S. I have just heard five pistol shots down street - as such things are in my line, I will go and see about it.

P. S. No 2 - 5 A.M. - The pistol did its work well - one man - a Jackson County Missourian, shot two of my friends, (police officers,) through the heart - both died within three minutes. Murderer's name is John Campbell.

The "Unreliable" of this letter was a rival reporter on whom Mark Twain had conferred this name during the legislative session. His real name was Rice, and he had undertaken to criticize Clemens's reports. The brisk reply that Rice's letters concealed with a show of parliamentary knowledge a "festering mass of misstatements the author of whom should be properly termed the 'Unreliable," fixed that name upon him for life. This burlesque warfare delighted the frontier and it did not interfere with friendship. Clemens and Rice were constant associates, though continually firing squibs at each other in their respective papers - a form of personal journalism much in vogue on the Comstock.

In the next letter we find these two journalistic "blades" enjoying themselves together in the coast metropolis. This letter is labeled "No. 2," meaning, probably, the second from San Francisco, but No. 1 has disappeared, and even No, 2 is incomplete.

To Mrs. Jane Clemens and Mrs. Moffett, in St. Louis: No. 2 - ($20.00 Enclosed)

LICK HOUSE, S. F., June 1, '63.

MY DEAR MOTHER AND SISTER, - The Unreliable and myself are still here, and still enjoying ourselves. I suppose I know at least a thousand people here - a, great many of them citizens of San Francisco, but the majority belonging in Washoe - and when I go down Montgomery street, shaking hands with Tom, Dick and Harry, it is just like being in Main street in Hannibal and meeting the old familiar faces. I do hate to go back to Washoe. We fag ourselves completely out every day, and go to sleep without rocking, every night. We dine out and we lunch out, and we eat, drink and are happy - as it were. After breakfast, I don't often see the hotel again until midnight - or after. I am going to the Dickens mighty fast. I know a regular village of families here in the house, but I never have time to call on them. Thunder! we'll know a little more about this town, before we leave, than some of the people who live in it. We take trips across the Bay to Oakland, and down to San Leandro, and Alameda, and those places;

and we go out to the Willows, and Hayes Park, and Fort Point, and up to Benicia; and yesterday we were invited out on a yachting excursion, and had a sail in the fastest yacht on the Pacific Coast. Rice says: "Oh, no - we are not having any fun, Mark - Oh, no, I reckon not - it's somebody else - it's probably the 'gentleman in the wagon'!" (popular slang phrase.) When I invite Rice to the Lick House to dinner, the proprietors send us champagne and claret, and then we do put on the most disgusting airs. Rice says our calibre is too light - we can't stand it to be noticed!

I rode down with a gentleman to the Ocean House, the other day, to see the sea horses, and also to listen to the roar of the surf, and watch the ships drifting about, here, and there, and far away at sea. When I stood on the beach and let the surf wet my feet, I recollected doing the same thing on the shores of the Atlantic - and then I had a proper appreciation of the vastness of this country - for I had traveled from ocean to ocean across it.

(Remainder missing.)

Not far from Virginia City there are some warm springs that constantly send up jets of steam through fissures in the mountainside. The place was a health resort, and Clemens, always subject to bronchial colds, now and again retired there for a cure.

A letter written in the late summer - a gay, youthful document - belongs to one of these periods of convalescence.

To Mrs. Jane Clemens and Mrs. Moffett, in St. Louis: No. 12 - $20 enclosed.

STEAMBOAT SPRINGS, August 19, '63.

MY DEAR MOTHER AND SISTER, - Ma, you have given my vanity a deadly thrust. Behold, I am prone to boast of having the widest reputation, as a local editor, of any man on the Pacific coast, and you gravely come forward and tell me "if I work hard and attend closely to my business, I may aspire to a place on a big San Francisco daily, some day." There's a comment on human vanity for you! Why, blast it, I was under the impression that I could get such a situation as that any time I asked for it. But I don't want it. No paper in the United States can afford to pay me what my place on the "Enterprise" is worth. If I were not naturally a lazy, idle, good-for-nothing vagabond, I could make it pay me $20,000 a year. But I don't suppose I shall ever be any account. I lead an easy life, though, and I don't care a cent whether school keeps or not. Everybody knows me, and I fare like a prince wherever I go, be it on this side of the mountains or the other. And I am proud to say I am the most conceited ass in the Territory.

You think that picture looks old? Well, I can't help it - in reality I am not as old as I was when I was eighteen.

I took a desperate cold more than a week ago, and I seduced Wilson (a Missouri boy, reporter of the Daily

Union,) from his labors, and we went over to Lake Bigler. But I failed to cure my cold. I found the "Lake House" crowded with the wealth and fashion of Virginia, and I could not resist the temptation to take a hand in all the fun going. Those Virginians - men and women both - are a stirring set, and I found if I went with them on all their eternal excursions, I should bring the consumption home with me - so I left, day before yesterday, and came back into the Territory again. A lot of them had purchased a site for a town on the Lake shore, and they gave me a lot. When you come out, I'll build you a house on it. The Lake seems more supernaturally beautiful now, than ever. It is the masterpiece of the Creation.

The hotel here at the Springs is not so much crowded as usual, and I am having a very comfortable time of it. The hot, white steam puffs up out of fissures in the earth like the jets that come from a steam-boat's 'scape pipes, and it makes a boiling, surging noise like a steam-boat, too-hence the name. We put eggs in a handkerchief and dip them in the springs - they "soft boil" in 2 Minutes, and boil as hard as a rock in 4 minutes. These fissures extend more than a quarter of a mile, and the long line of steam columns looks very pretty. A large bath house is built over one of the springs, and we go in it and steam ourselves as long as we can stand it, and then come out and take a cold shower bath. You get baths, board and lodging, all for $25 a week - cheaper than living in Virginia without baths.....

Yrs aft

MARK.

It was now the autumn of 1863. Mark Twain was twenty-eight years old. On the Coast he had established a reputation as a gaily original newspaper writer. Thus far, however, he had absolutely no literary standing, nor is there any evidence that he had literary ambitions; his work was unformed, uncultivated - all of which seems strange, now, when we realize that somewhere behind lay the substance of immortality. Rudyard Kipling at twenty-eight had done his greatest work.

Even Joseph Goodman, who had a fine literary perception and a deep knowledge of men, intimately associated with Mark Twain as he was, received at this time no hint of his greater powers. Another man on the staff of the Enterprise, William Wright, who called himself "Dan de Quille," a graceful humorist, gave far more promise, Goodman thought, of future distinction.

It was Artemus Ward who first suspected the value of Mark Twain's gifts, and urged him to some more important use of them. Artemus in the course of a transcontinental lecture tour, stopped in Virginia City, and naturally found congenial society on the Enterprise staff. He had intended remaining but a few days, but lingered three weeks, a period of continuous celebration, closing only with the holiday season. During one night of final festivities, Ward slipped away and gave a performance on his own account. His letter to Mark Twain, from Austin, Nevada, written a day or two later, is most characteristic.

Artemus Ward's letter to Mark Twain:

AUSTIN, Jan. 1, '64.

MY DEAREST LOVE, - I arrived here yesterday a.m. at 2 o'clock. It is a wild, untamable place, full of lionhearted boys. I speak tonight. See small bills.

Why did you not go with me and save me that night? - I mean the night I left you after that dinner party. I went and got drunker, beating, I may say, Alexander the Great, in his most drinkinist days, and I blackened my face at the Melodeon, and made a gibbering, idiotic speech. God-dam it! I suppose the Union will have it. But let it go. I shall always remember Virginia as a bright spot in my existence, as all others must or rather cannot be, as it were.

Love to Jo. Goodman and Dan. I shall write soon, a powerfully convincing note to my friends of "The Mercury." Your notice, by the way, did much good here, as it doubtlessly will elsewhere. The miscreants of the Union will be batted in the snout if they ever dare pollute this rapidly rising city with their loathsome presence.

Some of the finest intellects in the world have been blunted by liquor.

Do not, sir - do not flatter yourself that you are the only chastely-humorous writer onto the Pacific slopes.

Good-bye, old boy - and God bless you! The matter of which I spoke to you so earnestly shall be just as earnestly attended to - and again with very many warm regards for Jo. and Dan., and regards to many of the good friends we met.

I am Faithfully, gratefully yours,

ARTEMUS WARD.

The Union which Ward mentions was the rival Virginia. City paper; the Mercury was the New York Sunday Mercury, to which he had urged Mark Twain to contribute. Ward wrote a second letter, after a siege of illness at Salt Lake City. He was a frail creature, and three years later, in London, died of consumption. His genius and encouragement undoubtedly exerted an influence upon Mark Twain. Ward's second letter here follows.

Artemus Ward to S. L. Clemens:

SALT LAKE CITY, Jan. 21, '64.

MY DEAR MARK, - I have been dangerously ill for the past two weeks here, of congestive fever. Very grave fears were for a time entertained of my recovery, but happily the malady is gone, though leaving me very, very weak. I hope to be able to resume my journey in a week or so. I think I shall speak in the Theater here, which is one of the finest establishments of the kind in America.

The Saints have been wonderfully kind to me, I could not have been better or more tenderly nursed at home - God bless them!

I am still exceedingly weak - can't write any more. Love to Jo and Dan, and all the rest. Write me at St. Louis.

Always yours,

ARTEMUS WARD.

If one could only have Mark Twain's letters in reply to these! but they have vanished and are probably long since dust. A letter which he wrote to his mother assures us that he undertook to follow Ward's advice. He was not ready, however, for serious literary effort. The article, sent to the Mercury, was distinctly of the Comstock variety; it was accepted, but it apparently made no impression, and he did not follow it up.

For one thing, he was just then too busy reporting the Legislature at Carson City and responding to social demands. From having been a scarcely considered unit during the early days of his arrival in Carson Mark Twain had attained a high degree of importance in the little Nevada capital. In the Legislature he was a power; as correspondent for the Enterprise he was feared and respected as well as admired. His humor, his satire, and his fearlessness were dreaded weapons.

Also, he was of extraordinary popularity. Orion's wife, with her little daughter, Jennie, had come out from the

States. The Governor of Nevada had no household in Carson City, and was generally absent. Orion Clemens reigned in his stead, and indeed was usually addressed as "Governor" Clemens. His home became the social center of the capital, and his brilliant brother its chief ornament. From the roughest of miners of a year before he had become, once more, almost a dandy in dress, and no occasion was complete without him. When the two Houses of the Legislature assembled, in January, 1864, a burlesque Third House was organized and proposed to hold a session, as a church benefit. After very brief consideration it was decided to select Mark Twain to preside at this Third House assembly under the title of "Governor," and a letter of invitation was addressed to him. His reply to it follows:

To S. Pixley and G. A. Sears, Trustees:

CARSON CITY, January 23, 1864.

GENTLEMEN, Certainly. If the public can find anything in a grave state paper worth paying a dollar for, I am willing that they should pay that amount, or any other; and although I am not a very dusty Christian myself, I take an absorbing interest in religious affairs, and would willingly inflict my annual message upon the Church itself if it might derive benefit thereby. You can charge what you please; I promise the public no amusement, but I do promise a reasonable amount of instruction. I am responsible to the Third House only, and I hope to be permitted to make it exceedingly warm for that body, without caring whether the sympathies of the public and the Church be enlisted in their favor, and against myself, or not.

Respectfully,

MARK TWAIN.

There is a quality in this letter more suggestive of the later Mark Twain than anything that has preceded it. His Third House address, unfortunately, has not been preserved, but those who heard it regarded it as a classic. It probably abounded in humor of the frontier sort-unsparing ridicule of the Governor, the Legislature, and individual citizens. It was all taken in good part, of course, and as a recognition of his success he received a gold watch, with the case properly inscribed to "The Governor of the Third House." This was really his first public appearance in a field in which he was destined to achieve very great fame.

V. LETTERS 1864-66.

SAN FRANCISCO AND HAWAII

Life on the Comstock came to an end for Mark Twain in May, 1864. It was the time of The Flour Sack Sanitary Fund, the story of which he has told in Roughing It. He does not, however, refer to the troubles which this special fund brought upon himself. Coming into the Enterprise office one night, after a gay day of "Fund" celebration, Clemens wrote, for next day's paper, a paragraph intended to be merely playful, but which proved highly offending to certain ladies concerned with the flour-sack enterprise. No files of the paper exist today, so we cannot judge of the quality of humor that stirred up trouble.

The trouble, however, was genuine enough, Virginia's rival paper seized upon the chance to humiliate its enemy, and presently words were passed back and forth until nothing was left to write but a challenge. The story of this duel, which did not come off, has been quite fully told elsewhere, both by Mark Twain and the present writer; but the following letter - a revelation of his inner feelings in the matter of his offense - has never before been published.

To Mrs. Cutler, in Carson City:

VIRGINIA, May 23rd, 1864.

MRS. W. K. CUTLER:

MADAM, - I address a lady in every sense of the term. Mrs. Clemens has informed me of everything that has occurred in Carson in connection with that unfortunate item of mine about the Sanitary Funds accruing from the ball, and from what I can understand, you are almost the only lady in your city who has understood the circumstances under which my fault was committed, or who has shown any disposition to be lenient with me. Had the note of the ladies been properly worded, I would have published an ample apology instantly - and possibly I might even have done so anyhow, had that note arrived at any other time - but it came at a moment when I was in the midst of what ought to have been a deadly quarrel with the publishers of the Union, and I could not come out and make public apologies to any one at such a time. It is bad policy to do it even now (as challenges have already passed between myself and a proprietor of the Union, and the matter is still in abeyance,) but I suppose I had better say a word or two to show the ladies that I did not wilfully and maliciously do them a wrong.

But my chief object, Mrs. Cutler, in writing you this note (and you will pardon the liberty I have taken,) was to thank you very kindly and sincerely for the consideration you have shown me in this matter, and for your continued friendship for Mollie while others are disposed to withdraw theirs on account of a fault for which I alone am responsible.

Very truly yours,

SAM. L. CLEMENS.

The matter did not end with the failure of the duel. A very strict law had just been passed, making it a felony even to send or accept a challenge. Clemens, on the whole, rather tired of Virginia City and Carson, thought it a good time to go across the mountains to San Francisco. With Steve Gillis, a printer, of whom he was very fond - an inveterate joker, who had been more than half responsible for the proposed duel, and was to have served as his second - he took the stage one morning, and in due time was in the California metropolis, at work on the Morning Call.

Clemens had been several times in San Francisco, and loved the place. We have no letter of that summer, the first being dated several months after his arrival. He was still working on the Call when it was written, and contributing literary articles to the Californian, of which Bret Harte, unknown to fame, was editor. Harte had his office just above the rooms of the Call, and he and Clemens were good friends. San Francisco had a real literary group that, for a time at least, centered around the offices of the Golden Era. In a letter that follows Clemens would seem to have scorned this publication, but he was a frequent contributor to it at one period. Joaquin Miller was of this band of literary pioneers; also Prentice Mulford, Charles Warren Stoddard, Fitzhugh Ludlow, and Orpheus C. Kerr.

To Mrs. Jane Clemens and Mrs. Moffett, in St. Louis:

Sept. 25, 1864.

MY DEAR MOTHER AND SISTER, - You can see by my picture that this superb climate agrees with me. And it ought, after living where I was never out of sight of snow peaks twenty-four hours during three years. Here we have neither snow nor cold weather; fires are never lighted, and yet summer clothes are never worn - you wear spring clothing the year round.

Steve Gillis, who has been my comrade for two years, and who came down here with me, is to be married, in a week or two, to a very pretty girl worth $130,000 in her own right - and then I shall be alone again, until they build a house, which they will do shortly.

We have been here only four months, yet we have changed our lodgings five times, and our hotel twice. We are very comfortably fixed where we are, now, and have no fault to find with the rooms or with the people - we are the only lodgers in a well-to-do private family, with one grown daughter and a piano in the parlor adjoining our room. But I need a change, and must move again. I have taken rooms further down the street. I shall stay in this little quiet street, because it is full of gardens and shrubbery, and there are none but dwelling houses in it.

I am taking life easy, now, and I mean to keep it up for awhile. I don't work at night any more. I told the "Call" folks to pay me $25 a week and let me work only in daylight. So I get up at ten every morning, and quit work at five or six in the afternoon. You ask if I work for greenbacks? Hardly. What do you suppose I could do with greenbacks here?

I have engaged to write for the new literary paper - the "Californian" - same pay I used to receive on the "Golden Era" - one article a week, fifty dollars a month. I quit the "Era," long ago. It wasn't high-toned enough. The "Californian" circulates among the highest class of the community, and is the best weekly literary paper in the United States - and I suppose I ought to know.

I work as I always did - by fits and starts. I wrote two articles last night for the Californian, so that lets me out for two weeks. That would be about seventy-five dollars, in greenbacks, wouldn't it?

Been down to San Jose (generally pronounced Sannozay - emphasis on last syllable) - today fifty miles from here, by railroad. Town of 6,000 inhabitants, buried in flowers and shrubbery. The climate is finer than ours here, because it is not so close to the ocean, and is protected from the winds by the coast range.

I had an invitation today, to go down on an excursion to San Luis Obispo, and from thence to the city of Mexico, to be gone six or eight weeks, or possibly longer, but I could not accept, on account of my contract to act as chief mourner or groomsman at Steve's wedding.

I have triumphed. They refused me and other reporters some information at a branch of the Coroner's office -

Massey's undertaker establishment, a few weeks ago. I published the wickedest article on them I ever wrote in my life, and you can rest assured we got all the information we wanted after that.

By the new census, San Francisco has a population of 130,000. They don't count the hordes of Chinamen.

Yrs aftly,

SAM.

I send a picture for Annie, and one for Aunt Ella - that is, if she will have it.

Relations with the Call ceased before the end of the year, though not in the manner described in Roughing It. Mark Twain loved to make fiction of his mishaps, and to show himself always in a bad light. As a matter of fact, he left the Call with great willingness, and began immediately contributing a daily letter to the Enterprise, which brought him a satisfactory financial return.

In the biographical sketch with which this volume opens, and more extendedly elsewhere, has been told the story of the trouble growing out of the Enterprise letters, and of Mark Twain's sojourn with James Gillis in the Tuolumne Hills. Also how, in the frowsy hotel at Angel's Camp, he heard the frog anecdote that would become the corner-stone of his fame. There are no letters of this period - only some note-book entries. It is probable that he did not write home, believing, no doubt, that he had very little to say.

For more than a year there is not a line that has survived. Yet it had been an important year; the jumping frog story, published in New York, had been reprinted East and West, and laughed over in at least a million homes. Fame had not come to him, but it was on the way.

Yet his outlook seems not to have been a hopeful one.

To Mrs. Jane Clemens and Mrs. Moffett, in St. Louis:

SAN FRANCISCO, Jan. 20, 1866.

MY DEAR MOTHER AND SISTER, - I do not know what to write; my life is so uneventful. I wish I was back there piloting up and down the river again. Verily, all is vanity and little worth - save piloting.

To think that, after writing many an article a man might be excused for thinking tolerably good, those New York people should single out a villainous backwoods sketch to compliment me on! "Jim Smiley and His Jumping Frog" - a squib which would never have been written but to please Artemus Ward, and then it reached New York too late to appear in his book.

But no matter. His book was a wretchedly poor one, generally speaking, and it could be no credit to either of us to appear between its covers.

This paragraph is from the New York correspondence of the San Francisco Alta:

(Clipping pasted in.)

"Mark Twain's story in the Saturday Press of November 18th, called 'Jim Smiley and His Jumping Frog,' has set all New York in a roar, and he may be said to have made his mark. I have been asked fifty times about it and its author, and the papers are copying it far and near. It is voted the best thing of the day. Cannot the Californian afford to keep Mark all to itself? It should not let him scintillate so widely without first being filtered through the California press."

The New York publishing house of Carleton & Co. gave the sketch to the Saturday Press when they found it was too late for the book.

Though I am generally placed at the head of my breed of scribblers in his part of the country, the place properly belongs to Bret Harte, I think, though he denies it, along with the rest. He wants me to club a lot of old sketches together with a lot of his, and publish a book. I wouldn't do it, only he agrees to take all the trouble. But I want to know whether we are going to make anything out of it, first. However, he has written to a New York publisher, and if we are offered a bargain that will pay for a month's labor we will go to work and prepare the volume for the press.

Yours affy,

SAM.

Bret Harte and Clemens had by this time quit the Californian, expecting to contribute to Eastern periodicals. Clemens, however, was not yet through with Coast journalism. There was much interest just at this time in the Sandwich Islands, and he was selected by the foremost Sacramento paper to spy out the islands and report aspects and conditions there. His letters home were still infrequent, but this was something worth writing.

To Mrs. Jane Clemens and Mrs. Moffett, in St. Louis:

SAN FRANCISCO, March 5th, 1866.

MY DEAR MOTHER AND SISTER, - I start to do Sandwich Islands day after tomorrow, (I suppose Annie is geographer enough by this time to find them on the map), in the steamer "Ajax." We shall arrive there in about twelve days. My friends seem determined that I shall not lack acquaintances, for I only decided today to go, and they have already sent me letters of introduction to everybody down there worth knowing. I am to remain there a month and ransack the islands, the great cataracts and the volcanoes completely, and write twenty or thirty letters to the Sacramento Union - for which they pay me as much money as I would get if I staid at home.

If I come back here I expect to start straight across the continent by way of the Columbia river, the Pend d'Oreille Lakes, through Montana and down the Missouri river, - only 200 miles of land travel from San Francisco to New Orleans.

Goodbye for the present.

Yours,

SAM.

His home letters from the islands are numerous enough; everything there being so new and so delightful that he found joy in telling of it; also, he was still young enough to air his triumphs a little, especially when he has dined with the Grand Chamberlain and is going to visit the King!

The languorous life of the islands exactly suited Mask Twain. All his life he remembered them - always planning to return, some day, to stay there until he died. In one of his note-books he wrote: "Went with Mr. Dam to his cool, vine-shaded home; no care-worn or eager, anxious faces in this land of happy contentment. God, what a contrast with California and the Washoe!"

And again:

Oh, Islands there are on the face of the deep
Where the leaves never fade and the skies never weep."

The letters tell the story of his sojourn, which stretched itself into nearly five months.

To Mrs. Jane Clemens and Mrs. Moffett, in St. Louis:

HONOLULU, SANDWICH ISLANDS,
April 3, 1866.

MY DEAR MOTHER AND SISTER, - I have been here two or three weeks, and like the beautiful tropical climate better and better. I have ridden on horseback all over this island (Oahu) in the meantime, and have visited all the ancient battle-fields and other places of interest. I have got a lot of human bones which I took from one of these battle-fields - I guess I will bring you some of them. I went with the American Minister and took dinner this evening with the King's Grand Chamberlain, who is related to the royal family, and although darker than a mulatto, he has an excellent English education and in manners is an accomplished gentleman. The dinner was as ceremonious as any I ever attended in California - five regular courses, and five kinds of wine and one of brandy. He is to call for me in the morning with his carriage, and we will visit the King at the palace - both are good Masons - the King is a Royal Arch Mason. After dinner tonight they called in the "singing girls," and we had some beautiful music; sung in the native tongue.

The steamer I came here in sails tomorrow, and as soon as she is gone I shall sail for the other islands of the group and visit the great volcano - the grand wonder of the world. Be gone two months.

Yrs.

SAM.

To Mrs. Jane Clemens and Mrs. Moffett, in St. Louis:

WAILUKU SUGAR PLANTATION,
ISLAND OF MAUI, H. I., May 4,1866.

MY DEAR MOTHER AND SISTER, - 11 O'clock at night. - This is the infernalist darkest country, when the moon don't shine; I stumbled and fell over my horse's lariat a minute ago and hurt my leg, so I must stay here tonight.

I got the same leg hurt last week; I said I hadn't got hold of a spirited horse since I had been on the island, and one of the proprietors loaned me a big vicious colt; he was altogether too spirited; I went to tighten the cinch before mounting him, when he let out with his left leg (?) and kicked me across a ten-acre lot. A native rubbed and doctored me so well that I was able to stand on my feet in half an hour. It was then half after four and I had an appointment to go seven miles and get a girl and take her to a card party at five.

I have been clattering around among the plantations for three weeks, now, and next week I am going to visit the extinct crater of Mount Haleakala - the largest in the world; it is ten miles to the foot of the mountain; it rises 10,000 feet above the valley; the crater is 29 miles in circumference and 1,000 feet deep. Seen from the summit, the city of St. Louis would look like a picture in the bottom of it.

As soon as I get back from Haleakala (pronounced Hally-ekka-lah) I will sail for Honolulu again and thence to the Island of Hawaii (pronounced Hah-wy-ye,) to see the greatest active volcano in the world - that of Kilauea (pronounced Kee-low-way-ah) - and from thence back to San Francisco - and then, doubtless, to the States. I have been on this trip two months, and it will probably be two more before I get back to California.

Yrs affy

SAM.

He was having a glorious time - one of the most happy, carefree adventures of his career. No form of travel or undertaking could discountenance Mark Twain at thirty.

To Mrs. Orion Clemens, in Carson City:

HONOLULU, May 22, 1866.

MY DEAR SISTER, - I have just got back from a sea voyage - from the beautiful island of Maui, I have spent five weeks there, riding backwards and forwards among the sugar plantations - looking up the splendid scenery and visiting the lofty crater of Haleakala. It has been a perfect jubilee to me in the way of pleasure.

I have not written a single line, and have not once thought of business, or care or human toil or trouble or sorrow or weariness. Few such months come in a lifetime.

I set sail again, a week hence, for the island of Hawaii, to see the great active volcano of Kilauea. I shall not get back here for four or five weeks, and shall not reach San Francisco before the latter part of July.

So it is no use to wait for me to go home. Go on yourselves.

If I were in the east now, I could stop the publication of a piratical book which has stolen some of my sketches.

It is late-good-bye, Mollie,

Yr Bro

SAM.

To Mrs. Jane Clemens and Mrs. Moffett, in St. Louis:

HONOLULU, SANDWICH ISLANDS,
June 21,1866.

MY DEAR MOTHER AND SISTER, - I have just got back from a hard trip through the Island of Hawaii, begun on the 26th of May and finished on the 18th of June - only six or seven days at sea - all the balance horse-back, and the hardest mountain road in the world. I staid at the volcano about a week and witnessed the greatest eruption that has occurred for years. I lived well there. They charge $4 a day for board, and a dollar or two extra for guides and horses. I had a pretty good time. They didn't charge me anything. I have got back sick - went to bed as soon as I arrived here - shall not be strong again for several days yet. I rushed too fast. I ought to have taken five or six weeks on that trip.

A week hence I start for the Island of Kauai, to be gone three weeks and then I go back to California.

The Crown Princess is dead and thousands of natives cry and wail and dance and dance for the dead, around the King's Palace all night and every night. They will keep it up for a month and then she will be buried.

Hon. Anson Burlingame, U. S. Minister to China, and Gen. Van Valkenburgh, Minister to Japan, with their families and suites, have just arrived here en route.

They were going to do me the honor to call on me this morning, and that accounts for my being out of bed now. You know what condition my room is always in when you are not around - so I climbed out of bed and dressed and shaved pretty quick and went up to the residence of the American Minister and called on them. Mr. Burlingame told me a good deal about Hon. Jere Clemens and that Virginia Clemens who was wounded in a duel. He was in Congress years with both of them. Mr. B. sent for his son, to introduce him - said he could tell that frog story of mine as well as anybody. I told him I was glad to hear it for I never tried to tell it myself without making a botch of it. At his request I have loaned Mr. Burlingame pretty much everything I ever wrote. I guess he will be an almighty wise man by the time he wades through that lot.

If the New United States Minister to the Sandwich Islands (Hon. Edwin McCook,) were only here now, so that I could get his views on this new condition of Sandwich Island politics, I would sail for California at once. But he will not arrive for two weeks yet and so I am going to spend that interval on the island of Kauai.

I stopped three days with Hon. Mr. Cony, Deputy Marshal of the Kingdom, at Hilo, Hawaii, last week and by a funny circumstance he knew everybody that I ever knew in Hannibal and Palmyra. We used to sit up all night talking and then sleep all day. He lives like a Prince. Confound that Island! I had a streak of fat and a streak of lean all over it - got lost several times and had to sleep in huts with the natives and live like a dog.

Of course I couldn't speak fifty words of the language. Take it altogether, though, it was a mighty hard trip.

Yours Affect.

SAM.

Burlingame and Van Valkenburgh were on their way to their posts, and their coming to the islands just at this time proved a most important circumstance to Mark Twain. We shall come to this presently, in a summary of the newspaper letters written to the Union. June 27th he wrote to his mother and sister a letter, only a fragment of which survives, in which he tells of the arrival in Honolulu of the survivors of the ship Hornet, burned on the line, and of his securing the first news report of the lost vessel.

Part of a letter to Mrs. Jane Clemens and Mrs. Moffett, in St. Louis:

HONOLULU, June 27, 1866 .

. . . with a gill of water a day to each man. I got the whole story from the third mate and two of the sailors. If my account gets to the Sacramento Union first, it will be published first all over the United States, France, England, Russia and Germany - all over the world; I may say. You will see it. Mr. Burlingame went with me all the time, and helped me question the men - throwing away invitations to dinner with the princes and foreign dignitaries, and neglecting all sorts of things to accommodate me. You know how I appreciate that kind of thing - especially from such a man, who is acknowledged to have no superior in the diplomatic circles of the world, and obtained from China concessions in favor of America which were refused to Sir Frederick Bruce and Envoys of France and Russia until procured for them by Burlingame himself - which service was duly acknowledged by those dignitaries. He hunted me up as soon as he came here, and has done me a hundred favors since, and says if I will come to China in the first trip of the great mail steamer next January and make his house in Pekin my home, he will afford me facilities that few men can have there for seeing and learning. He will give me letters to the chiefs of the great Mail Steamship Company which will be of service to me in this matter. I expect to do all this, but I expect to go to the States first - and from China to the Paris World's Fair.

Don't show this letter.

Yours affly

   SAM.

P. S. The crown Princess of this Kingdom will be buried tomorrow with great ceremony - after that I sail in two weeks for California.

This concludes Mark Twain's personal letters from the islands. Of his descriptive news letters there were about twenty, and they were regarded by the readers of the Union as distinctly notable. Re-reading those old letters to-day it is not altogether easy to understand why. They were set in fine nonpareil type, for one thing, which present-day eyes simply refuse at any price, and the reward, by present-day standards, is not especially tempting.

The letters began in the Union with the issue of April the 16th, 1866. The first - of date March 18th - tells of the writer's arrival at Honolulu. The humor in it is not always of a high order; it would hardly pass for humor today at all. That the same man who wrote the Hawaiian letters in 1866 (he was then over thirty years old) could, two years later, have written that marvelous book, the Innocents Abroad, is a phenomenon in literary development.

The Hawaiian letters, however, do show the transition stage between the rough elemental humor of the Comstock and the refined and subtle style which flowered in the Innocents Abroad. Certainly Mark Twain's genius was finding itself, and his association with the refined and cultured personality of Anson Burlingame undoubtedly aided in that discovery. Burlingame pointed out his faults to him, and directed him to a better way. No more than that was needed at such a time to bring about a transformation.

The Sandwich Islands letters, however, must have been precisely adapted to their audience - a little more refined than the log Comstock, a little less subtle than the Atlantic public - and they added materially to his Coast prestige. But let us consider a sample extract from the first Sandwich Islands letter:

Our little band of passengers were as well and thoughtfully cared for by the friends they left weeping upon the wharf, as ever were any similar body of pilgrims. The traveling outfit conferred upon me began with a naval uniform, continued with a case of wine, a small assortment of medicinal liquors and brandy, several boxes of cigars, a bunch of matches, a fine-toothed comb, and a cake of soap, and ended with a pair of socks. (N. B. I gave the soap to Brown, who bit into it, and then. shook his head and said that, as a general thing, he liked to prospect curious, foreign dishes, and find out what they were made of, but he couldn't go that, and threw it overboard.)

It is nearly impossible to imagine humor in this extract, yet it is a fair sample of the entire letter.

He improves in his next, at least, in description, and gives us a picture of the crater. In this letter, also, he writes well and seriously, in a prophetic strain, of the great trade that is to be established between San Francisco and Hawaii, and argues for a line of steamers between the ports, in order that the islands might be populated by Americans, by which course European trade in that direction could be superseded. But the humor in this letter, such as it is, would scarcely provoke a smile to-day.

As the letters continue, he still urges the fostering of the island trade by the United States, finds himself impressed by the work of the missionaries, who have converted cannibals to Christians, and gives picturesque bits of the life and scenery.

Hawaii was then dominated chiefly by French and English; though the American interests were by no means small.

Extract from letter No. 4:

Cap. Fitch said "There's the king. That's him in the buggy. I know him as far as I can see him."

I had never seen a king, and I naturally took out a note-book and put him down: "Tall, slender, dark, full-bearded; green frock-coat, with lapels and collar bordered with gold band an inch wide; plug hat, broad gold band around it; royal costume looks too much like livery; this man is not as fleshy as I thought he was."

I had just got these notes when Cap. Fitch discovered that he'd got hold of the wrong king, or rather, that he'd got hold of the king's driver, or a carriage driver of one of the nobility. The king wasn't present at all. It was a great disappointment to me. I heard afterwards that the comfortable, easy-going king, Kamehameha V., had been seen sitting on a barrel on the wharf, the day before, fishing. But there was no consolation in that. That did not restore me my lost king.

This has something of the flavor of the man we were to know later; the quaint, gentle resignation to disappointment which is one of the finest touches in his humor.

Further on he says: "I had not shaved since I left San Francisco. As soon as I got ashore I hunted up a striped pole, and shortly found one. I always had a yearning to be a king. This may never be, I suppose, but, at any rate, it will always be a satisfaction to me to know that, if I am not a king, I am the next thing to it. I have been shaved by the king's barber."

Honolulu was a place of cats. He saw cats of every shade and variety. He says: "I saw cats - tomcats, Mary-Ann cats, bobtailed cats, blind cats, one-eyed cats, wall-eyed cats, cross-eyed cats, gray cats, black cats, white cats, yellow cats, striped cats, spotted cats, tame cats, wild cats, singed cats, individual cats, groups of cats, platoons of cats, companies of cats, armies of cats, multitudes of cats, millions of cats, and all of them sleek, fat, and lazy, and sound asleep." Which illustrates another characteristic of the humor we were to know later - the humor of grotesque exaggeration, in which he was always strong.

He found the islands during his periods of inaction conducive to indolence. "If I were not so fond of looking into the rich mass of green leaves," he says, "that swathe the stately tamarind right before my door, I would idle less, and write more, I think."

The Union made good use of his letters. Sometimes it printed them on the front page. Evidently they were popular from the beginning. The Union was a fine, handsome paper - beautiful in its minute typography, and in its press-work; more beautiful than most papers of to-day, with their machine-set type, their vulgar illustrations, and their chain-lightning presses. A few more extracts:

"The only cigars here are those trifling, insipid, tasteless, flavorless things they call Manilas - ten for twenty-five cents - and it would take a thousand of them to be worth half the money. After you have smoked about thirty-five dollars' worth of them in the forenoon, you feel nothing but a desperate yearning to go out somewhere and take a smoke. "

"Captains and ministers form about half the population. The third fourth is composed of Kanakas and mercantile foreigners and their families. The final fourth is made up of high officers of the Hawaiian government, and there are just about enough cats to go round. "

In No. 6, April the 2d, he says: "An excursion to Diamond Head, and the king's cocoanut grove, was planned to-day, at 4.30 P. M., the party to consist of half a dozen gentlemen and three ladies. They all started at the appointed hour except myself. Somebody remarked that it was twenty minutes past five o'clock, and that woke me up. It was a fortunate circumstance that Cap. Phillips was there with his 'turn-out,' as he calls his top buggy that Cap. Cook brought here in 1778, and a horse that was here when Cap. Cook came. "

This bit has something the savor of his subsequent work, but, as a rule, the humor compares poorly with that which was to come later.

In No. 7 he speaks of the natives singing American songs - not always to his comfort. "Marching Through Georgia" was one of their favorite airs. He says: "If it had been all the same to Gen. Sherman, I wish he had gone around by the way of the Gulf of Mexico, instead of marching through Georgia. "

Letters Nos. 8, 9, and 10 were not of special importance. In No. 10 he gives some advice to San Francisco as to the treatment of whalers. He says:

"If I were going to advise San Francisco as to the best strategy to employ in order to secure the whaling trade, I should say, 'Cripple your facilities for "pulling" sea captains on any pretence that sailors can trump up, and show the whaler a little more consideration when he is in port.'"

In No. 11, May 24th, he tells of a trip to the Kalehi Valley, and through historic points. At one place he looked from a precipice over which old Kamehameha I. drove the army of Oahu, three-quarters of a century before.

The vegetation and glory of the tropics attracted him. "In one open spot a vine of a species unknown had taken possession of two tall dead stumps, and wound around and about them, and swung out from their tops, and twined their meeting tendrils together into a faultless arch. Man, with all his art, could not improve upon its symmetry."

He saw Sam Brannan's palace, "The Bungalow," built by one Shillaber of San Francisco at a cost of from thirty to forty thousand dollars. In its day it had outshone its regal neighbor, the palace of the king, but had fallen to decay after passing into Brannan's hands, and had become a picturesque Theban ruin by the time of Mark Twain's visit.

In No. 12, June 20th (written May 23d), he tells of the Hawaiian Legislature, and of his trip to the island of Maui, where, as he says, he never spent so pleasant a month before, or bade any place good-by so regretfully.

In No. 13 he continues the Legislature, and gives this picture of Minister Harris: "He is six feet high, bony and rather slender; long, ungainly arms; stands so straight he leans back a little; has small side whiskers; his head long, up and down; he has no command of language or ideas; oratory all show and pretence; a big washing and a small hang-out; weak, insipid, and a damn fool in general."

In No. 14, June 22d, published July 16th, he tells of the death and burial ceremonies of the Princess Victoria K. K., and, what was to be of more importance to him, of the arrival of Anson Burlingame, U. S. Minister to China, and Gen. Van Valkenburgh, U. S. Minister to Japan. They were to stay ten or fourteen days, he said, but an effort would be made to have them stay over July 4th.

Speaking of Burlingame: "Burlingame is a man who could be esteemed, respected, and popular anywhere, no matter whether he was among Christians or cannibals." Then, in the same letter, comes the great incident. "A letter arrived here yesterday, giving a meagre account of the arrival, on the Island of Hawaii, of nineteen poor, starving wretches, who had been buffeting a stormy sea, in an open boat, for forty-three days. Their ship, the Hornet, from New York, with a quantity of kerosene on board had taken fire and burned in Lat. 2d. north, and Long. 35d. west. When they had been entirely out of provisions for a day or two, and the cravings of hunger become insufferable, they yielded to the ship-wrecked mariner's fearful and awful alternative, and solemnly drew lots to determine who of their number should die, to furnish food for his comrades; and then the morning mists lifted, and they saw land. They are being cared for at Sanpahoe (Not yet corroborated)."

The Hornet disaster was fully told in his letter of June 27th. The survivors were brought to Honolulu, and with the assistance of the Burlingame party, Clemens, laid up with saddle boils, was carried on a stretcher to the hospital, where, aided by Burlingame, he interviewed the shipwrecked men, securing material for the most important piece of serious writing he had thus far performed. Letter No. 15 to the Union - of date June 25th - occupied the most of the first page in the issue of July 19. It was a detailed account of the sufferings of officers and crew, as given by the third officer and members of the crew.

From letter No. 15:

In the postscript of a letter which I wrote two or three days ago, and sent by the ship "Live Yankee," I gave you the substance of a letter received here from Hilo, by Walker Allen and Co., informing them that a boat, containing fifteen men in a helpless and starving condition, had drifted ashore at Sanpahoe, Island of Hawaii, and that they had belonged to the clipper ship "Hornet" - Cap. Mitchell, master - had been afloat since the burning of that vessel, about one hundred miles north of the equator, on the third of May - forty-three days.

The Third Mate, and ten of the seamen have arrived here, and are now in the hospital. Cap. Mitchell, one seaman named Antonio Passene, and two passengers, Samuel and Henry Ferguson, of New York City, eighteen and twenty-eight years, are still at Hilo, but are expected here within the week. In the Captain's modest epitome of the terrible romance you detect the fine old hero through it. It reads like Grant.

Here follows the whole terrible narrative, which has since been published in more substantial form, and has been recognized as literature. It occupied three and a half columns on the front page of the Union, and, of course, constituted a great beat for that paper - a fact which they appreciated to the extent of one hundred dollars the column upon the writer's return from the islands.

In letters Nos. 14. and 15. he gives further particulars of the month of mourning for the princess, and funeral ceremonials. He refers to Burlingame, who was still in the islands. The remaining letters are unimportant.

The Hawaiian episode in Mark Twain's life was one of those spots that seemed to him always filled with sunlight. From beginning to end it had been a long luminous dream; in the next letter, written on the homeward-bound ship, becalmed under a cloudless sky, we realize the fitting end of the experience.

To Mrs. Jane Clemens and Mrs. Moffett, in St. Louis:

ON BOARD SHIP Smyrniote,
AT SEA, July 30, 1866.

DEAR MOTHER AND SISTER, - I write, now, because I must go hard at work as soon as I get to San Francisco, and then I shall have no time for other things - though truth to say I have nothing now to write which will be calculated to interest you much. We left the, Sandwich Islands eight or ten days - or twelve days ago - I don't know which, I have been so hard at work until today (at least part of each day,) that the time has slipped away almost unnoticed. The first few days we came at a whooping gait being in the latitude of the "North-east trades," but we soon ran out of them. We used them as long as they lasted-hundred of miles - and came dead straight north until exactly abreast of San Francisco precisely straight west of the city in a bee-line - but a long bee-line, as we were about two thousand miles at sea-consequently, we are not a hundred yards nearer San Francisco than you are. And here we lie becalmed on a glassy sea - we do not move an inch-we throw banana and orange peel overboard and it lies still on the water by the vessel's side. Sometimes the ocean is as dead level as the Mississippi river, and glitters glassily as if polished - but usually, of course, no matter how calm the weather is, we roll and surge over the grand ground-swell. We amuse ourselves tying pieces of tin to the ship's log and sinking them to see how far we can distinguish them under water - 86 feet was the deepest we could see a small piece of tin, but a white plate would show about as far down as the steeple of Dr. Bullard's church would reach, I guess. The sea is very dark and blue here.

Ever since we got becalmed - five days - I have been copying the diary of one of the young Fergusons (the two boys who starved and suffered, with thirteen others, in an open boat at sea for forty-three days, lately, after their ship, the "Hornet," was burned on the equator.) Both these boys, and Captain Mitchell, are passengers with us. I am copying the diary to publish in Harper's Magazine, if I have time to fix it up properly when I get to San Francisco.

I suppose, from present appearances, - light winds and calms, - that we shall be two or three weeks at sea, yet - and I hope so - I am in no hurry to go to work.

Sunday Morning, Aug. 6.

This is rather slow. We still drift, drift, drift along - at intervals a spanking breeze and then - drift again - hardly move for half a day. But I enjoy it. We have such snowy moonlight, and such gorgeous sunsets. And the ship is so easy - even in a gale she rolls very little, compared to other vessels - and in this calm we could dance on deck, if we chose. You can walk a crack, so steady is she. Very different from the Ajax. My trunk used to get loose in the stateroom and rip and tear around the place as if it had life in it, and I always had to take my clothes off in bed because I could not stand up and do it.

There is a ship in sight - the first object we have seen since we left Honolulu. We are still 1300 or 1400 miles from land and so anything like this that varies the vast solitude of the ocean makes all hands light-hearted and cheerful. We think the ship is the "Comet," which left Honolulu several hours before we did. She is about twelve miles away, and so we cannot see her hull, but the sailors think it is the Comet because of some peculiarity about her fore-top-gallant sails. We have watched her all the forenoon.

Afternoon We had preaching on the quarter-deck by Rev. Mr. Rising, of Virginia City, old friend of mine. Spread a flag on the booby-hatch, which made a very good pulpit, and then ranged the chairs on either side against the bulwarks; last Sunday we had the shadow of the mainsail, but today we were on the opposite tack, close hauled, and had the sun. I am leader of the choir on this ship, and a sorry lead it is. I hope they will have a better opinion of our music in Heaven than I have down here. If they don't a thunderbolt will come down and knock the vessel endways.

The other ship is the Comet - she is right abreast three miles away, sailing on our course - both of us in a dead calm. With the glasses we can see what we take to be men and women on her decks. I am well acquainted with nearly all her passengers, and being so close seems right sociable.

Monday 7 - I had just gone to bed a little after midnight when the 2d mate came and roused up the captain and said "The Comet has come round and is standing away on the other tack." I went up immediately, and so did all our passengers, without waiting to dress-men, women and children. There was a perceptible breeze. Pretty soon the other ship swept down upon us with all her sails set, and made a fine show in the luminous starlight. She passed within a hundred yards of us, so we could faintly see persons on her decks. We had two minutes' chat with each other, through the medium of hoarse shouting, and then she bore away to windward.

In the morning she was only a little black peg standing out of the glassy sea in the distant horizon - an almost invisible mark in the bright sky. Dead calm. So the ships have stood, all day long - have not moved 100 yards.

Aug. 8 - The calm continues. Magnificent weather. The gentlemen have all turned boys. They play boyish games on the poop and quarter-deck. For instance: They lay a knife on the fife-rail of the mainmast - stand off three steps, shut one eye, walk up and strike at it with the fore-finger; (seldom hit it;) also they lay a knife on the deck and walk seven or eight steps with eyes close shut, and try to find it. They kneel - place elbows against knees - extend hands in front along the deck - place knife against end of fingers - then clasp hands behind back and bend forward and try to pick up the knife with their teeth and rise up from knees without rolling over or losing their balance. They tie a string to the shrouds - stand with back against it walk three steps (eyes shut) - turn around three times and go and put finger on the string; only a military man can do it. If you want to know how perfectly ridiculous a grown man looks performing such absurdities in the presence of ladies, get one to try it.

Afternoon - The calm is no more. There are three vessels in sight. It is so sociable to have them hovering about us on this broad waste of water. It is sunny and pleasant, but blowing hard. Every rag about the ship is spread to the breeze and she is speeding over the sea like a bird. There is a large brig right astern of us with all her canvas set and chasing us at her best. She came up fast while the winds were light, but now it is hard to tell whether she gains or not. We can see the people on the forecastle with the glass. The race is exciting. I am sorry to know that we shall soon have to quit the vessel and go ashore if she keeps up this speed.

Friday, Aug. 10 - We have breezes and calms alternately. The brig is two miles to three astern, and just stays there. We sail directly east - this brings the brig, with all her canvas set, almost in the eye of the sun, when it sets - beautiful. She looks sharply cut and black as a coal, against a background of fire and in the midst of a sea of blood.

San Francisco, Aug. 20. - We never saw the Comet again till the 13th, in the morning, three miles away. At three o'clock that afternoon, 25 days out from Honolulu, both ships entered the Golden Gate of San Francisco side by side, and 300 yards apart. There was ˙a gale blowing, and both vessels clapped on every stitch of canvas and swept up through the channel and past the fortresses at a magnificent gait.

I have been up to Sacramento and squared accounts with the Union. They paid me a great deal more than they promised me.

Yrs aff

SAM.

VI. LETTERS 1866-67.

THE LECTURER. SUCCESS ON THE COAST. IN NEW YORK. THE GREAT OCEAN EXCURSION

It was August 13th when he reached San Francisco and wrote in his note-book, "Home again. No - not home again - in prison again, and all the wild sense of freedom gone. City seems so cramped and so dreary with toil and care and business anxieties. God help me, I wish I were at sea again!"

The transition from the dreamland of a becalmed sailing-vessel to the dull, cheerless realities of his old life, and the uncertainties of his future, depressed him - filled him with forebodings. At one moment he felt himself on the verge of suicide - the world seemed so little worth while.

He wished to make a trip around the world, a project that required money. He contemplated making a book of his island letters and experiences, and the acceptance by Harper's Magazine of the revised version of the Hornet Shipwreck story encouraged this thought.

Friends urged him to embody in a lecture the picturesque aspect of Hawaiian life. The thought frightened him, but it also appealed to him strongly.

He believed he could entertain an audience, once he got started on the right track. As Governor of the Third House at Carson City he had kept the audience in hand. Men in whom he had the utmost confidence insisted that he follow up the lecture idea and engage the largest house in the city for his purpose. The possibility of failure appalled him, but he finally agreed to the plan.

In Roughing It, and elsewhere, has been told the story of this venture - the tale of its splendid success. He was no longer concerned, now, as to his immediate future. The lecture field was profitable. His audience laughed and shouted. He was learning the flavor of real success and exulting in it. With Dennis McCarthy, formerly one of the partners in the Enterprise, as manager, he made a tour of California and Nevada.

To Mrs. Jane Clemens and others, in St. Louis:

VIRGINIA CITY, Nov. 1, 1866.

ALL THE FOLKS, AFFECTIONATE GREETING, - You know the flush time's are past, and it has long been impossible to more than half fill the Theatre here, with any sort of attraction, but they filled it for me, night before last - full - dollar all over the house.

I was mighty dubious about Carson, but the enclosed call and some telegrams set that all right - I lecture there tomorrow night.

They offer a full house and no expense in Dayton - go there next. Sandy Baldwin says I have made the most sweeping success of any man he knows of.

I have lectured in San Francisco, Sacramento, Marysville, Grass Valley, Nevada, You Bet, Red Dog and Virginia. I am going to talk in Carson, Gold Hill, Silver City, Dayton, Washoe, San Francisco again, and again here if I have time to re-hash the lecture.

Then I am bound for New York - lecture on the Steamer, maybe.

I'll leave toward 1st December - but I'll telegraph you. Love to all.

Yrs.

MARK.

His lecture tour continued from October until December, a period of picturesque incident, the story of which has been recorded elsewhere. - [See Mark Twain: A Biography, by the same author] - It paid him well; he could go home now, without shame. Indeed, from his next letter, full of the boyish elation which always to his last years was the complement of his success, we gather that he is going home with special honors - introductions from ministers and the like to distinguished personages of the East.

To Mrs. Jane Clemens and family, in St. Louis:

SAN F., Dec. 4, 1866.

MY DEAR FOLKS, - I have written to Annie and Sammy and Katie some time ago - also, to the balance of you.

I called on Rev. Dr. Wadsworth last night with the City College man, but he wasn't at home. I was sorry, because I wanted to make his acquaintance. I am thick as thieves with the Rev. Stebbings, and I am laying for the Rev. Scudder and the Rev. Dr. Stone. I am running on preachers, now, altogether. I find them gay. Stebbings is a regular brick. I am taking letters of introduction to Henry Ward Beecher, Rev. Dr. Tyng, and other eminent parsons in the east. Whenever anybody offers me a letter to a preacher, now I snaffle it on the spot. I shall make Rev. Dr. Bellows trot out the fast nags of the cloth for me when I get to New York. Bellows is an able, upright and eloquent man - a man of imperial intellect and matchless power - he is Christian in the truest sense of the term and is unquestionably a brick....

Gen. Drum has arrived in Philadelphia and established his head-quarters there, as Adjutant Genl. to Maj. Gen. Meade. Col. Leonard has received a letter from him in which he offers me a complimentary benefit if I will come there. I am much obliged, really, but I am afraid I shan't lecture much in the States.

The China Mail Steamer is getting ready and everybody says I am throwing away a fortune in not going in her. I firmly believe it myself.

I sail for the States in the Opposition steamer of the 5th inst., positively and without reserve. My room is already secured for me, and is the choicest in the ship. I know all the officers.

Yrs. Affy

MARK.

We get no hint of his plans, and perhaps he had none. If his purpose was to lecture in the East, he was in no hurry to begin. Arriving in New York, after an adventurous voyage, he met a number of old Californians - men who believed in him - and urged him to lecture. He also received offers of newspaper engagements, and from Charles Henry Webb, who had published the Californian, which Bret Harte had edited, came the proposal to collect his published sketches, including the jumping Frog story, in book form. Webb himself was in New York, and offered the sketches to several publishers, including Canton, who had once refused the Frog story by omitting it from Artemus Ward's book. It seems curious that Canton should make a second mistake and refuse it again, but publishers were wary in those days, and even the newspaper success of the Frog story did not tempt him to venture it as the title tale of a book. Webb finally declared he would publish the book himself, and Clemens, after a few weeks of New York, joined his mother and family in St. Louis and gave himself up to a considerable period of visiting, lecturing meantime in both Hannibal and Keokuk.

Fate had great matters in preparation for him. The Quaker City Mediterranean excursion, the first great ocean picnic, was announced that spring, and Mark Twain realized that it offered a possible opportunity for him to see something of the world. He wrote at once to the proprietors of the Alta-California and proposed that they send him as their correspondent. To his delight his proposition was accepted, the Alta agreeing to the twelve hundred dollars passage money, and twenty dollars each for letters.

The Quaker City was not to sail until the 8th of June, but the Alta wished some preliminary letters from New York. Furthermore, Webb had the Frog book in press, and would issue it May 1st. Clemens, therefore, returned to New York in April, and now once more being urged by the Californians to lecture, he did not refuse. Frank Fuller, formerly Governor of Utah, took the matter in hand and engaged Cooper Union for the venture. He timed it for May 6th, which would be a few days after the appearance of Webb's book. Clemens was even more frightened at the prospect of this lecture than he had been in San Francisco, and with more reason, for in New York his friends were not many, and competition for public favor was very great. There are two letters written May 1st, one to his people, and one to Bret Harte, in San Francisco; that give us the situation.

www.ingramcontent.com/pod-product-compliance
Lightning Source LLC
Chambersburg PA
CBHW051825170626

46807CB00003B/1026